D0251962

About this Book

'There is no alternative' – to neoliberal economics, the Americanization of the world's economies, and globalization. This remains the driving assumption within the international development policy establishment. In this book, two economists, Ha-Joon Chang and Ilene Grabel, cogently explain this dominant school's main assertions about how economies develop and the policies that all countries ought to pursue. The authors then combine data and a devastating economic logic with an analysis of the historical experiences of leading Western and East Asian economies during their development, in order to question the validity of the neo-liberal development model.

Turning to policy, the authors set out concrete, practical alternatives to neoliberalism across the key economic areas: trade and industrial policy; privatization; intellectual property rights; external borrowing, portfolio and foreign direct investment; domestic financial regulation; and management of exchange rates, central banking and monetary policy, and government revenue and expenditure. In doing so, they advocate the most useful proposals that have emerged around the world along with some innovative measures of their own.

This empowering and accessible book seeks to be of practical useful-ness to students of development and to those, in government and beyond, looking for concrete policy ideas. The hope is that it will stimulate discussion of the ways in which development policies can be reclaimed by those seeking to promote rapid economic growth that is equitable, stable and sustainable.

Critical Praise for this Book

This unusually well-written, direct and succinct book describes neo-liberal positions fairly; offers theoretically rigorous and empirically accurate critiques; and describes feasible, practical alternative policies that take realistic account of political, economic and financial con-straints. Discussion of financial, monetary, fiscal, trade and industry policy and intellectual property rights is especially strong and con-structive and makes important, innovative contributions. It is a fine, carefully analytical achievement which would contribute to hastening both efficient and socially just development wherever the insights are appropriately used.

John Langmore, Representative of the ILO to the UN

Chang and Grabel demolish the 'myths' (or fabrications) underlying neoliberal views about economic development and provide succinct, constructive suggestions for policies regarding trade and industry, privatization and intellectual property rights, private capital movements, financial regulation, and macroeconomics. *Reclaiming Development* is a manifesto that should be on the shelves of policymakers, academics, and students worldwide.

Lance Taylor, Arnhold Professor, New School University,
author of *Reconstructing Macroeconomics*

A growing number of developing countries are taking back control over economic policy from the IMF and the World Bank. The wide range of policy suggestions contained in this book provides a rich mine of concrete and practicable alternatives from which to choose in taking advantage of whatever room globalization still allows developing countries and reshaping economic policy in their own interests.

Martin Khor, Director, Third World Network

This book is not only a superb antidote to the numbing myths of neoliberalism but also a cogent and stimulating presentation of the many possibilities for alternatives to neoliberal economic policy that both theory and history provide policymakers and students of development.

Thandika Mkandawire, Director, United Nations
Research Institute for Social Development (UNRISD)

The dominant neoliberal economic doctrine asserts that there is no alternative to its policy prescriptions which provide the foundations for success in an age of globalization. This book questions and refutes the belief system implicit in the assertion.

Its real achievement is that it goes beyond a mere critique of neoliberal policies. The authors are to be commended for providing a range of concrete and feasible alternatives in critical policy areas based not only on successful real world examples but also on the latest economic theories.

The book is a rich mixture of theory, history and reality. The outcome is a reader-friendly text that is both accessible and lively. It will enhance and broaden our understanding of current debates on economic policies in the wider context of globalization and development.

Deepak Nayyar, Vice-Chancellor, University of Delhi

Reclaiming Development

An Alternative Economic Policy Manual

Ha-Joon Chang and Ilene Grabel

Fernwood Publishing
Nova Scotia

Books for Change
Bangalore

World Book Publishing
Beirut

SIRD
Kuala Lumpur

TWN
Penang

David Philip
Cape Town

ZED BOOKS
London & New York

Reclaiming Development was first published in 2004 by

In Canada: Fernwood Publishing Ltd,
8422 St Margaret's Bay Road (Hwy 3) Site 2A, Box 5,
Black Point, Nova Scotia, BOJ 1BO

In India: Books for Change,
139 Richmond Road, Bangalore 560 025

In Lebanon, Bahrain, Egypt, Jordan, Kuwait, Qatar, Saudi Arabia and United Arab Emirates: World Book Publishing, 282 Emile Eddeh Street,
Ben Salem bldg, PO Box 3176, Beirut, Lebanon www.wbpbooks.com

In Malaysia: Strategic Information Research Development (SIRD),
No. 11/4E, Petaling Jaya, 46200 Selangor

Third World Network (TWN), 121-S Jalan Utama, 10450 Penang

In Southern Africa: David Philip (an imprint of New Africa Books),
99 Garfield Road, Claremont 7700, South Africa

In the rest of the world: Zed Books Ltd,
7 Cynthia Street, London N1 9JF, UK
and Room 400, 175 Fifth Avenue, New York, NY 10010, USA
www.zedbooks.co.uk

Second impression 2005

Copyright © Ha-Joon Chang and Ilene Grabel 2004

The right of Ha-Joon Chang and Ilene Grabel to be identified as the authors of this work has been asserted by them in accordance with the Copyright, Designs and Patents Act, 1988

Designed and typeset in Monotype Garamond by Illuminati, Grosmont
Cover designed by Andrew Corbett
Printed and bound in EU by Cox & Wyman, Reading

Distributed in the USA exclusively by Palgrave Macmillan, a division of St Martin's Press, LLC, 175 Fifth Avenue, New York, NY 10010

A catalogue record for this book is available from the British Library
Library of Congress Cataloging-in-Publication Data available
Canadian CIP data available from the National Library of Canada

Canada 1 55266 138 5 Pb
India 81 87380 97 7 Pb
Lebanon 9953 14 052 9 Pb
Malaysia (SIRD) 983 2535 30 1 Pb
Malaysia (TWN) 983 2729 27 0 Pb
South Africa 0 86486 658 5 Pb

Zed 1 84277 200 7 (Hb)
Zed 1 84277 201 5 (Pb)

Contents

List of Abbreviations

CEO	Chief executive officer
ECLAC	Economic Commission for Latin America and the Caribbean
ERP	Economic Report of the [US] President
EPZs	Export processing zones
FTAA	Free trade area of the Americas
FTZs	Free trade zones
FDI	Foreign direct investment
GATT	General Agreement on Tariffs and Trade
HDR	Human Development Report
ISI	Import-substituting industrialization
IPRs	Intellectual property rights
IMF	International Monetary Fund
ILO	International Labour Organization
LTCM	Long-Term Capital Management
MNCs	Multinational corporations
NIH	National Institute of Health
NICs	Newly industrializing countries
NGO	Nongovernmental organization
NAFTA	North American Free Trade Agreement
OECD	Organization for Economic Cooperation and Development
PI	Portfolio investment
R&D	Research and development
SOEs	State-owned enterprises
SAPs	Structural adjustment programmes
TRIPS	Trade-related aspects of intellectual property rights

TNCs	Transnational corporations
UN	United Nations
UNDP	United Nations Development Programme
VAT	Value-added tax
WTO	World Trade Organization

Acknowledgements

This book would not have been written without the encouragement and advice of Robert Molteno, our wonderful editor at Zed.

Duncan Green read the first draft of all the main chapters and provided many useful comments on them. George DeMartino reviewed several drafts of the manuscript, and his comments improved each version immeasurably.

Ha-Joon Chang wishes to thank the Korea Research Foundation, which through its BK21 programme supported his visit to the Department of Economics of Korea University, where he was a visiting research professor when the manuscript was finalized.

Ilene Grabel thanks the Faculty Research Fund of the University of Denver for the financial support that aided her work on this book, and Peter Zawadzki for his superb research assistance. She also thanks her wonderful students at the Graduate School of International Studies at the University of Denver and her friends in nongovernmental organizations for their insistence that she think about concrete policy alternatives to neoliberalism.

For Hee-Jeong and George

Introduction

Reclaiming Development

'There is no alternative.' This is the famous pronouncement by former British Prime Minister Margaret Thatcher when she was faced with widespread opposition to her programme of radical neoliberal reform during the 1980s. Thatcher's dictum captures the triumphalism, hubris and closed-mindedness with which the neoliberal orthodoxy has dominated discussions of economic policy around the world during the last quarter of a century.

This book begins with the premiss that the 'no alternative' dictum is fundamentally and dangerously incorrect. As we demonstrate in great detail throughout the book, feasible alternatives to neoliberal policies exist that can promote rapid economic development that is equitable, stable and sustainable. Some of these are proposals for strategies not yet adopted, to be sure. But many others have already proven their worth in practice across the globe. We offer them here in order to shatter the idea that there is no alternative, and to contribute to the vigorous campaign now underway across the globe to 'reclaim development'.

The timing of this book is propitious for three reasons. First, there is now abundant and increasing evidence that the economic policies associated with the neoliberal agenda have failed to achieve their chief goals, and have introduced serious problems, especially in the developing world. Second, there is a great deal of historical and current evidence that there are multiple routes to development. We argue that successful development is the result of diverse types of economic policies, the majority of which run counter to the policies advocated by neoliberal economists today. Third, at the present juncture the unbridled confidence of neoliberal economists seems to be faltering. In fact, a good deal has been published of late by neoliberal economists who tell us that they have grown disenchanted with certain aspects of the neoliberal policies embodied in what is commonly known as the 'Washington Consensus'. This apparent 'rethinking' of the development agenda has led some commentators to identify an emergent 'post-Washington Consensus' or 'post-neoliberal' policy agenda. Prominent examples include the book by Pedro-Paul Kuczynski and John Williamson titled *After the Washington Consensus* (2003) and a much-discussed study of financial globalization by a team of International Monetary Fund (IMF) economists (Prasad et al., 2003).

There are reasons to be encouraged by efforts to rethink development policy by key architects of the original Washington Consensus policies.[1] However, the spin on this new work inaccurately claims that the architects of the Washington Consensus have now 'seen the light', and have genuinely moved to a new way of thinking that transcends their previous policy prescriptions. This, in fact, is not at all the case. Instead, this new way of thinking merely seeks to save the core tenets of the Washington Consensus from embarrassment and refutation by modifying a few of its less central policy prescriptions. Indeed, the new thinking reaffirms and even extends its neoliberal character in several important policy domains (such as the increased attention that is paid to the promotion of labour market flexibility). Harvard University economist Dani Rodrik (2002) has aptly coined the term 'Augmented Washington Consensus' to refer to work along these lines.

This book seeks to provide real alternatives to the Washington Consensus – augmented or otherwise – in the developing world. *Our goal is nothing short of 'Reclaiming Development' from the neoliberal orthodoxy that has dominated discussions of development policy during the last quarter of a century.* We explain how and why neoliberal policies have failed developing countries, and demonstrate that there exists a range of achievable and desirable policy alternatives.

We begin the book in Part I by presenting and rejecting the six major 'Development Myths' that are used to justify the neoliberal policies that have been pursued with such disastrous results in the developing world during the last quarter of a century (Chapters 1–6). Part II is the heart of the book. Here we provide activists, policymakers and students of development policy with an array of concrete policy options that are superior to their neoliberal counterparts. In these chapters we look specifically at policies towards trade and industry (Chapter 7), privatization and intellectual property rights (Chapter 8), foreign bank borrowing and portfolio and foreign direct investment (Chapter 9), domestic financial regulation (Chapter 10), and exchange rates and currencies, central banking and monetary policy, and government revenue and expenditure (Chapter 11). In each case, we explain why the neoliberal policy recommendations in these domains have failed, often with disastrous consequences for developing countries. We then counterpose an array of alternative policies that can promote faster economic development than can neoliberalism, while ensuring that it is equitable and sustainable.

We must emphasize at the outset that we present this range of proposals in the spirit of pluralism and humility. We do not share the hubris of neoliberals, and therefore do not argue that there is an ideal, single approach to 'good' policy. We hope that this work will contribute to the promising new search within developing countries, multilateral agencies, nongovernmental organizations (NGOs) and activist communities for alternatives to neoliberal policy regimes.

We hope that this book is an antidote to the defeatism found among many opponents of neoliberalism who do not challenge these policies, believing that there are no credible alternatives. We also hope that our book empowers those who seek concrete alternatives to neoliberal policy. Towards these ends, we present our ideas in a clear and accessible manner so that both busy policymakers and those with little formal training in economics can make use of this book. However, the book is not simply a 'beginners' guide' to development policy. Professional economists will also find that our arguments are firmly grounded – even if plainly argued – in frontier research in development economics.

Our greatest hope for this book is that it is useful, empowering and accessible. We hope that it stimulates discussion of the ways that development policies can be reclaimed by those seeking to promote rapid economic development around the world that is equitable, stable and sustainable.

Note

1. In particular, we are pleased that recent work by neoliberals recognizes that unrestrained flows of liquid international capital can lead to speculative bubbles and financial crises in developing countries.

Part I

Myths and Realities about Development

The chapters in Part I examine six distinct, but related, 'Development Myths'. These myths form the basis of today's conventional wisdom regarding the types of economic policies and institutions that are both appropriate and feasible for developing countries. This discussion serves as the backdrop for our discussion of economic policy alternatives in Part II.

Each of these chapters begins with a brief statement of a development myth as it is generally articulated ('The Myth'). This is followed by an explication of the arguments that advocates generally advance in support of the myth ('The Myth Explored'). Finally, each chapter concludes with a detailed refutation of the myth ('The Myth Rejected').

Myth 1

'Today's wealthy countries achieved success through a steadfast commitment to the free market'

1.1 The Myth

Today's industrialized countries have prospered because of their steadfast commitment to free-market economic policies. Unfortunately, many policymakers in developing countries today have failed to learn this lesson, and remain committed to state interventionism. But the laws of economics and history cannot be denied, and this approach is doomed to failure.

1.2 The Myth Explored

The rich countries prospered through free trade and free financial flows.

Many economists argue that countries like Britain and the USA became world economic leaders because of their vigorous commitment to free-market policies.[1] These policies promote market- rather than state-direction of trade and financial flows. This strategy minimizes the scope of government regulation while encouraging private ownership of resources, enterprises and even ideas.

In this view, nineteenth-century France lost ground to Britain as a dominant player on the world scene because of its notoriously

meddlesome government. Similarly, the Japanese economy has suffered from slow growth over the last decade because its leaders
failed to liberalize the country's state-led economy.

The folly of state intervention is most dramatically illustrated
by the failed interlude of trade protectionism in industrialized
countries in the early twentieth century. Following Britain's success with free trade during and since the eighteenth century, most
of today's industrialized countries had adopted free-trade policies
by the 1870s. Free trade inaugurated an era of unprecedented
economic growth that extended until 1913.

Sadly, this free trade era ended with World War I and the
ensuing economic and political instability. In this context, governments ceded to pressures for protectionism. The Great Depression
exacerbated this trend: during the 1930s, governments erected a
variety of tariff barriers against one another and implemented
other 'beggar-thy-neighbour' strategies in a vain effort to promote
domestic growth and stability. The protectionist, nationalist direction of trade policy ultimately prolonged the Depression, undermined the world trading system, and fuelled the flames of fascism
in Europe. These economic, social and political tensions – the
consequence in part of the retreat from the market – contributed
significantly to the outbreak of World War II.

Today's industrialized countries returned to free-trade policies
following the end of World War II. Since then they have pursued
trade liberalization through the General Agreement on Trade
and Tariffs (GATT) and more recently through the World Trade
Organization (WTO). In parallel fashion, they also deregulated
and privatized their domestic industries. These initiatives have
promoted world prosperity, especially in developing countries.

A similar story applies to finance. Over the last two centuries or so, today's industrialized countries gradually learned
of the benefits of deregulated, market-mediated (domestic and
international) capital flows. 'Financial liberalization' has many
components, including market allocation of investment funds,
protection of investor rights and freedoms, and the maintenance

of transparency. The trend towards financial liberalization has been reversed from time to time, but today most industrialized countries are deeply committed to the market mediation of financial flows – domestically and internationally.

> Developing countries have suffered because of policymakers' proclivity to adopt interventionist economic policies.

With the attainment of independence, most developing countries adopted highly interventionist economic strategies. As a consequence, they have faced economic stagnation.

Interventionism had many components. Pursuing 'infant industry protection' and 'import-substituting industrialization' (ISI) policies, governments insulated domestic industries from foreign competition with steep tariffs, restrictive quotas and large subsidies. Governments also nationalized key industries, creating state-owned enterprises (SOEs), and heavily regulated private-sector firms. Moreover, governments manipulated investment by nationalizing banks, regulating domestic financial activities, and restricting cross-border capital flows.

Most developing countries maintained these interventionist policies until the early 1980s. By then, however, these policies were recognized to be a resounding failure. Infant industry protection had not achieved the objective of promoting internationally competitive mature industries. SOEs also fared poorly: state subsidies and insulation from market competition left them bloated, inefficient and dependent on the state. Financial markets were stunted, while financial institutions provided funds to otherwise nonviable firms. In addition, industrial and financial controls gave rise to widespread corruption, bureaucratic 'red tape', and a costly misallocation of entrepreneurial talents. Together, these policies induced huge budget deficits and international debts, rapid inflation and myriad economic dislocations.

The economic crisis that swept through the developing world in the 1980s was the direct result of these misguided policies.

The crisis led policymakers to embrace free-market capitalism – and not a moment too soon.

1.3 **The Myth Rejected**

The 'secret' of their success: today's industrialized countries did not become rich through free trade and free financial flows.

An honest reading of the historical record shows that today's industrialized countries pioneered and relied upon myriad interventionist industrial, trade and financial policies in the early and often in the later stages of their own development (see Chapters 7–11 and Chang 2002). With respect to trade, Britain and the USA, the most strident free-trade missionaries in the world today, actively utilized protectionist policy during the early years of their development. Indeed, they exercised greater protection than even Germany and France, countries typically associated with trade protection and industrial regulation. In the eighteenth century, for instance, Britain introduced import protection and export promotion policies to challenge the industrial supremacy of the Netherlands and Belgium (see Chapter 7) – policies that Japan and others would utilize so effectively in the decades after World War II.

The prize for protectionism, however, goes to the USA! It had the most protected economy in the world between the mid-nineteenth century and World War II (only Russia, for a brief period in the early twentieth century, maintained a more protected economy). The USA was also the intellectual home of infant industry protection, a strategy later adopted so successfully by Germany and Japan (see Chapter 7).

Most of today's industrialized countries also used aggressive industrial policy to rebuild and modernize their economies after the devastation of World War II, even while they liberalized trade. Industrial policy played an especially important role in the post-World War II economic transformation of Japan, France, Norway,

Austria and Finland. State-owned enterprises were also important during this period in France, Austria and Norway. Indeed, even the USA relies upon industrial policy, though it is not identified as such. For example, massive state investment and support for research and development (R&D) in defence and pharmaceuticals and large agricultural subsidies are de facto industrial policies with significant private-sector spillovers.[2] The development of transistors, radar, computers, nuclear fission, laser technology and the Internet can be traced directly to defence-related subsidies by the federal government.

Industrialized countries also used a variety of interventionist financial policies during the post-World War II period, and to great effect. These countries suffered from incessant financial instability prior to World War II because many then had neither central banks nor effective financial regulations. The financial stability (and ensuing growth) of the post-World War II era was very much a product of the effective financial regulation that characterized this era.

During the post-World War II era, Japan and most continental European countries subordinated their financial sectors to the needs of industrial development and thereby achieved rapid industrial growth. For example, the French government (via the central bank which it controlled) ensured that industrial policy objectives were met by the financial system. The Japanese government (working through the central bank and the Ministry of Finance) ensured that strategic industrial sectors received sufficient finance at attractive prices.

As we shall see in Chapter 9, almost all industrialized nations maintained stringent controls on international capital movements from the end of World War II until about 1980. These policies, known as capital controls, were designed to promote economic development and to protect fragile economies from the instability caused by capital flight. The USA was nearly alone in its failure to maintain capital controls following World War II (except for a brief moment in the early 1960s). The absence of capital controls in the USA was largely the product of the country's unique status as the world's financial superpower.

Finally, even while proclaiming the virtues of the free market, policymakers in industrialized countries have been quite willing to intervene in and re-regulate markets to avert financial crisis and/or to protect national (or sectoral) interest. Indeed, the US government has acted to socialize financial and economic risk on many recent occasions. Examples include its rescue of the Chrysler Corporation in 1980, and the multi-billion-dollar, publicly funded bail-outs of the savings and loan banks in 1989, the hedge fund Long-Term Capital Management (LTCM) in 1998, and the airline industry in 2001. In each of these cases, the government was willing to sacrifice the discipline of free financial markets in order to promote financial stability and to restore investor confidence.

The truth about developing countries: well-designed programmes of intervention explain most success stories.

As discussed in Chapter 2, the vast majority of developing countries performed far better in the post-World War II era of interventionism than in the post-1980 era of free-market policies. Indeed, the performance of developing countries during the interventionist era was impressive not only in an absolute sense, but also relative to the performance of today's industrialized countries at a comparable stage in their development.

The truly dismal period of developing country performance was prior to World War II. During this period, developing countries were often coerced into using extreme free-market policies by colonial powers or, when nominally independent, through treaties that deprived them of tariff autonomy and the right to have a central bank. The typical result was sluggish growth and even economic decline. Economic performance in developing countries only improved after World War II because independence in some countries and a supportive ideological climate enabled policymakers to pursue interventionist strategies.

This is not to say that state intervention always works. There are cases where state intervention failed spectacularly. But when we look at the most dramatic success stories, the record clearly shows that development success is strongly related to myriad types of interventionism. Indeed, except for the case of Hong Kong, the East Asian 'miracle' was engineered by activist 'developmental states' that aggressively promoted economic development and financial stability (see Woo-Cumings 1999). China and India have also developed successfully via strong state direction of economic affairs (see Chapters 5, 7–11).

Notes

1. This policy regime was then known as 'liberalism'. In its modern form it is called 'neoliberalism'. This concept is explored more carefully in Chapter 2.

2. Throughout the post-World War II period, between half and two-thirds of US R&D was supported by the federal government (Mowery and Rosenberg 1993: Table 2.3). In 1989, 46.4 per cent of US R&D was supported by the government, while only 16.4 per cent of Japanese R&D in the same year was government supported (Odagiri and Goto 1993: Table 3.3). This contrast is rather striking, especially given the widely held view of Japanese state interventionism.

2 Myth 2
'Neoliberalism works'

2.1 The Myth

Over the past two decades, those developing countries that adopted the neoliberal agenda have prospered, while those that continued to pursue state-directed economic models have stagnated. The lesson is clear: neoliberalism represents the sole path to development and prosperity.

2.2 The Myth Explored

Neoliberalism has succeeded where other regimes have failed.

The term 'neoliberalism' refers to the contemporary adoption of the free-market doctrines associated with the classical 'liberal' economists of the eighteenth and nineteenth centuries (such as Adam Smith and David Ricardo). The term 'Washington Consensus' is often used synonymously with neoliberalism because the US government, the International Monetary Fund (IMF) and the World Bank, all based in Washington DC, are such forceful advocates of these reforms.[1] They have been joined in the campaign to spread neoliberalism by the governments and business communities of many industrialized countries, and by many reformers within developing countries as well.

Neoliberalism has three chief components. It elevates the role of markets (over governments) in economic governance and in mediating flows of goods and capital (through the elimination of price supports and ceilings, free trade, market-determined exchange rates, etc.); it enhances the role and scope of the private sector and private property (through privatization, deregulation, etc.); and it promotes a particular notion of 'sound economic policy' (through balanced budgets, labour-market flexibility, low inflation, etc.).

These policies represent the *only* path to economic prosperity for developing countries in today's globalized world economy. Neoliberalism has dramatically improved growth performance, raised living standards, and promoted democracy and transparency throughout the world during the last two decades when these policies have been in place.

Two decades of neoliberalism demonstrate that it delivers results.

The neoliberal 'revolution' was motivated by the failure of the interventionist policies that were widely implemented from World War II through the 1970s. At the time, even while liberalizing international trade and financial flows, industrialized countries pursued Keynesian 'tax-and-spend' policies and heavily regulated their economies. Excessive government expenditure resulted in high inflation, low levels of savings, and discouraged private investment. High taxes, excessive social expenditure and extensive government regulation stifled private initiative. For their part, developing countries pursued other forms of interventionism, as we have seen. These policies, too, proved to be counterproductive and unsustainable.

The neoliberal revolution that began in the 1980s and that continues to unfold today has already generated tremendous benefits. The curtailment of the state has reduced budget deficits and inflationary pressures, and has promoted market competition, efficiency, private initiative and entrepreneurship. The incentives and opportunities introduced by neoliberalism have also promoted efficiency, savings, and domestic and foreign investment. Most importantly, neoliberalism has promoted rapid economic growth and improved living standards the world over.

Neoliberalism has also promoted democracy, good governance and sound economic policy in developing countries in several ways. First, the economic freedoms associated with the market economy undermine political autocracy and kleptocracy. Second, international investors generally shun countries with corrupt or autocratic regimes. Third, neoliberalism integrates governments and firms into the global community and thereby encourages the adoption of the norms of policy conduct and business practice associated with it.

But what are we to make of the series of financial crises that have rocked the developing world over the past two decades? These crises are evidence not of neoliberalism's failures but of the incompleteness of neoliberal reform. Crises indicate that governments continue to interfere in economic affairs – such as through government direction of credit to their 'clients', and through measures that insulate favoured investors from risk. The solution to this problem, then, is more neoliberalism, not less.

2.3 **The Myth Rejected**

> The record shows that neoliberalism has failed, even on its own terms. Neoliberalism has not delivered economic growth.

Putting the matter bluntly: roughly two decades of neoliberalism have failed miserably to generate economic growth. Harvard University economist Dani Rodrik (2002) cites dismal growth performance during the 1990s as the most damning evidence of the failure of neoliberalism. Only three countries, Argentina, Chile and Uruguay, grew faster during the neoliberal era of the 1990s than their historical average growth rates during the interventionist era of 1950–80. However, the Argentinean economy has since imploded, with devastating effects on its smaller neighbour Uruguay, largely because of the failure of its neoliberal policies. And Chilean success is at least partially attributable to 'non-orthodox' policies such as government subsidies to certain export industries (e.g. forestry) and, more importantly, to a stringent regime of capital controls during much of the 1990s (see Chapter 9.3).

In the industrialized countries, the annual growth rate of per capita income has fallen from about 3 per cent during the interventionist era of 1960–80 to 2 per cent during the neoliberal era of 1980–2000.[2] Developing countries have fared even worse. Their average annual per capita income growth slowed from 3 per cent during 1960–80 to 1.5 per cent during 1980–2000. Indeed, the median rate of per capita GDP growth in developing countries over the last two decades was zero. Most disturbing is the fact that the poorest developing countries (defined as countries with per capita GDP from $375 to $1,121) went from a modest 1.9 per cent rate of per capita GDP growth during the interventionist 1960s–80s to a *decline* of 0.5 per cent per year during the neoliberal era. In short, countries at every level of per capita GDP performed worse on average during the neoliberal era than in the two preceding decades.

Even these dismal statistics put too positive a spin on the achievements of neoliberalism. Growth rates in developing countries over the last two decades or so have been buttressed by the acceleration of economic growth in the two largest developing economies, namely China and India – countries that in no sense followed the neoliberal formula. During the neoliberal period, Latin America has virtually stopped growing, while sub-Saharan Africa has experienced negative growth, and many of the former Communist economies have simply collapsed. In Latin America and the Caribbean, for example, per capita GDP grew by only 7 per cent from 1980 to 2000. By contrast, per capita GDP for the same region grew by 75 per cent during 1960–80. The data for sub-Saharan African countries is even more startling: per capita GDP fell by about 15 per cent during 1980–2000, after having grown by about 34 per cent during 1960–80.

To summarize: two facts make it impossible to accept the claim that neoliberalism promotes economic growth. The best performing developing economies in the world today are highly interventionist, and the economic performance of developing countries as a whole has been decidedly worse during the neoliberal era than in the decades immediately preceding it.

> The growth failures of neoliberalism mean that it cannot even compensate for the other costs that it has introduced.

That neoliberalism does not deliver economic growth is just the beginning of the problem. Even worse is the fact that the anaemic growth achievements of this regime have been accompanied by numerous adverse consequences in other areas.

Neoliberals acknowledge that the transition to this regime induces short-term 'adjustment costs'. For instance, reductions in social spending may undermine living standards; reductions in government support for certain sectors may result in job losses; and so on. But neoliberals claim that these adjustment costs are transitory since the new environment provides attractive opportunities for adaptable individuals and firms to generate greater wealth. Additionally, neoliberals claim that the growth dividend induced by neoliberalism gives governments a means to compensate those who have temporarily lost ground. These claims do not stand up to scrutiny.

First, neoliberalism introduces new problems and aggravates existing ones, such as an increased vulnerability to banking, currency and generalized financial crises (Grabel 2002) and increased levels of inequality and poverty. These problems are long-lasting and hurt the majority of the population, especially in developing countries (see Chapters 7–11). Contrary to the claims of its advocates, neoliberalism is the root cause of these problems. Extending neoliberalism further cannot therefore be the solution.

Second, neoliberalism does not provide governments with the motivation or the means to compensate those who lose ground under this regime. This is the case for several reasons.

Neoliberalism is based on the premiss that the government bears minimal responsibility for social welfare since extensive social welfare policy would distort the incentives associated with the free market. The anti-inflationary bias of neoliberal policy also means that governments are not apt to engage in adequate social spending. Moreover, the groups that are disenfranchised economically by neoliberalism also generally lack sufficient political power to secure compensation from the government (DeMartino 2000). Even if appropriate political will for compensatory schemes existed, governments have few resources to expend for this purpose. This is because neoliberalism reduces the tax base, places a high priority on budget balance, and makes it difficult to tax internationally mobile firms and investors (see Chapter 11.3).

Neoliberalism aggravates inequality among and within nations.

Neoliberalism induces international unevenness and inequality rather than widespread growth. Most importantly, private capital flows tend to concentrate in those countries that have already inaugurated a virtuous cycle of growth, investment and rising productivity (see Chapter 9.1). Contrary to the neoliberal claim, foreign private capital inflows *follow rather than create rapid growth*. Taiwan, South Korea and China are exemplars of this process (and of the success of well-designed programmes of interventionism). Developing countries (especially the poorest of these) must therefore institute policies that initiate a sustainable growth path as a precondition for private capital inflows.

There are by now myriad studies demonstrating the clustering of productive economic activity and the associated concentration of private capital flows across the globe during the neoliberal period. Inward investment by multinational corporations (MNCs), termed foreign direct investment (or FDI), is representative of the broader trend. Contrary to economic theory, the majority of FDI is destined for capital-rich countries in the North rather than capital-poor countries of the South. In 2000, for instance, only

15.9 per cent of total world FDI and 5.5 per cent of total cross-border investment in financial assets, termed portfolio investment (PI), reached the South. Moreover, those flows that do reach the South are extremely concentrated.[3] In 2002, for example, China alone received about 37 per cent of all North–South FDI, while the top ten destination countries together received 70 per cent of the developing country total. In contrast, the far poorer countries of sub-Saharan Africa, where the need is unarguably the greatest, received only 4.9 per cent of total North–South FDI in that year (see Chapter 9.1).

Neoliberalism has induced rising inequality among countries, partly as a result of this concentration of private capital flows. The UNDP finds that in 1960 the countries with the richest 20 per cent of the world's population had aggregate income 30 times that of those countries with the poorest 20 per cent of the world's population. By 1980, at the beginning of the neoliberal era, that ratio had risen to 45 to 1; by 1989, it stood at 59 to 1; by 1997, it had risen to 70 to 1 (UNDP, 2001, 1999). In the neoliberal era, then, inequality between the richest and the poorest countries nearly doubled. This divergence is particularly apparent when one looks at the situation of sub-Saharan African countries. In 1960, per capita income in sub-Saharan Africa was about 11 per cent of per capita income in industrialized countries. By 1998, it had fallen to half that figure (UNDP, 2001: 16).

The neoliberal revolution has also deepened inequality within countries. A thorough empirical study of 73 countries by Cornia (2003) finds that 53 of them experienced a surge in income concentration over the last two decades. In regard to particular regions, Cornia concludes that: 'this increase [in income concentration] was universal in the economies in transition, almost universal in Latin America and the OECD and increasingly frequent, if less pronounced in the South, Southeast and East Asia' (2000: 9). He concludes that much of this increase in inequality within nations is due to various aspects of neoliberal reform (most importantly, liberalization of capital flows, domestic financial and labour markets, and tax reform).[4]

It is particularly notable that income inequality has grown faster in countries that have more fully embraced the neoliberal ideal, such as the USA and UK, than in those that have not (UNDP, 2001: 18). In the UK, the income share of the top 1 per cent nearly doubled from 5.37 per cent to 9.57 per cent between 1979 and 1998 (Atkinson 2002). In his study of the US economy, Paul Krugman observes that: '1 per cent of families in the US receive about 16 per cent of total pretax income, and have about 14 per cent of after-tax income. That share has roughly doubled over the last 30 years, and is now about as large as the share of the bottom 40 per cent of the population' (Krugman 2002: 67). Krugman also notes (citing a study by the Congressional Budget Office) that, 'between 1979 and 1997, the after-tax incomes of the top 1 per cent of families rose 157 per cent, compared with only a 10 per cent gain for families near the middle of the US income distribution' (64). More striking is the growing gap in the USA between the very rich, the shrinking middle class and the very poor.

We can compare the US record of increased inequality with the experience of Sweden, a country that has retained a good measure of social-democratic economic governance even while opening its economy to international trade and capital flows during this period. Again quoting Krugman:

> The median Swedish family has a standard of living roughly comparable with that of the median US family: wages are if anything higher in Sweden, and a higher tax burden is offset by public provision of health care and generally better public services. And as you move further down the income distribution, Swedish living standards are way ahead of those in the US. Swedish families that are ... poorer than 90% of the population have incomes 60% higher than their US counterparts. And very few people in Sweden experience the deep poverty that is all too common in the US. One measure: in 1994 only 6% of Swedes lived on less than $11 per day, compared with 14% in the US. (76)

> Poverty has risen in many regions of the developing world
> during the neoliberal era, and earlier progress in improving
> social conditions has been reversed.

Neoliberals often point out that the overall proportion of the world's population that lives in severe poverty has fallen over the last two decades. But they neglect to mention that this achievement is largely due to the strong economic performance of China and India, two countries that pursue distinctly non-neoliberal policies and collectively account for more than half of the world's poor.

Beyond China and India, poverty levels (according to a variety of measures) have risen in a great many countries during the neoliberal era. Today, the UNDP (2002: 2) reports that 2.8 billion people live on less than $2 per day, while 1.2 billion people live on less than $1 per day. In sub-Saharan Africa alone, half of the region's population is poorer now than in 1990 and 46 per cent of the population lives on less than $1 per day (UNDP, 2001: 10; 2002: 17). In South Asia, 40 per cent of the population now lives on less than $1 per day; the comparable figure is 15 per cent in East Asia, the Pacific and Latin America (UNDP 2001: 10). Moreover, progress in improving life expectancy and education and in reducing infant mortality was slower for a large number of countries during the neoliberal era as compared to the previous two decades (Weisbrot et al. 2001).

> Neoliberalism does not promote democracy. Indeed, in some
> important respects it undermines accountability, pluralism and
> national autonomy.

Finally, on the level of politics, neoliberalism is not associated with an increase in democracy or transparency. Evidence shows that the relationship between neoliberalism and democracy is far more complex than neoliberals recognize.

First, the market system is compatible with diverse political structures, ranging from repressive to democratic regimes. It does not necessarily serve as a corrosive on authoritarian regimes, as many neoliberals claim.

Second, global neoliberalism threatens democracy by granting global investors and corporations veto power over domestic policy choices that they oppose. A fundamental aspect of democratic governance entails the right of those affected by policy to participate meaningfully in decision-making. Under neoliberalism, however, owners of internationally mobile factors of production (particularly large investors and the wealthy) have secured increased 'veto power' over the legislative and policy domain (see Chapter 9). By affording these actors freedom to withdraw funds from those countries that pursue strategies that threaten their interests, global neoliberalism effectively erodes national policy autonomy (DeMartino 1999). This structural power need not be exercised to be effective; today large investors and firms can merely threaten to relocate as a means to block government and citizen initiatives that they oppose. Therefore the flight of investors, or even the threat thereof, serves as a powerful deterrent to expansionary or redistributive economic and social policies, and to policies that promote labour rights (including the right to form unions and bargain collectively).

Third, the increased frequency of financial crisis under neoliberalism has greatly increased the power of the IMF vis-à-vis national governments. IMF assistance comes with 'strings attached': critical domestic decisions are vetted by an institution that is dominated by the USA and serves the interests of the global financial community. Neoliberalism thus undermines pluralism and policy independence in developing countries.

Notes

1. Rodrik (2002) uses the term 'Augmented Washington Consensus' to reflect the numerous caveats that neoliberals now attach to this agenda, such as the need for good governance, anti-corruption measures, anti-poverty programmes, and, most notably, some control over

liquid, international capital flows. Kuczynski and Williamson (2003) are an exemplar of this perspective. They emphasize that they do not reject the original Washington Consensus, but rather claim that 'the way forward is to complete, correct, and complement the [neoliberal] reforms of a decade ago, not to reverse them' (18). But, especially in practice, this new consensus still gives pride of place to widespread liberalization (especially in labour, currency and product markets) and fiscal discipline over other goals. This was demonstrated forcefully during the IMF's 2001–02 negotiations with Argentina and Brazil when it conditioned financial assistance on the traditional package of neoliberal reforms.

2. Data in this and the next paragraph are from Weisbrot et al. 2001. See also Chang (2002: ch. 4) on the growth failures of neoliberalism.

3. All data in this paragraph are taken from World Bank (various years).

4. For consistent findings on transition economies and Asia, see UNDP 1999: 36; for Latin America, where 83.8 per cent of the population live in countries with worsening inequality, see ECLAC 2002: 83.

3 **Myth 3**

'Neoliberal globalization cannot and should not be stopped'

3.1 **The Myth**

Globalization is an inevitable, unstoppable force that promises tremendous rewards. Policymakers, especially in developing countries, must learn to cope with and respond to globalization by embracing neoliberal economic policies if they are to promote economic security and prosperity.

3.2 **The Myth Explored**

Globalization is driven by technological progress.

Globalization is the result of the revolutions in communication and transportation that began in the nineteenth century. Starting with the invention of the telegraph and the steamship, technologies of transport and communication have progressed relentlessly, drawing various parts of the world ever closer.[1] It took the early US settlers several months to sail across the Atlantic in the early seventeenth century; it took several weeks for early steamships to make the crossing in the nineteenth century; and it takes only three hours for supersonic aircraft to traverse this distance today. Prior to the long-distance telegraph, it took five weeks to send a message from London to Bombay. Long-distance telegraphs reduced transmission time to minutes (Standgate 1999: 97), and the Internet has made communication almost instantaneous.

Each advance in communications and transport technology changes the nature of business and production. It is only natural that entrepreneurs would look beyond their national borders for profitable opportunities and new markets made accessible by new technologies. Transportation costs are so low today that Japan can import coal from Australia; Sweden can import furniture parts from India; and Europe can import bottled water from Canada. The Internet has increased the speed and efficiency of international business since it reduces the need for face-to-face contact among executives. Finnish firms can arrange to outsource their production to Taiwan and Chileans can export smoked salmon to Korea based upon deals arranged over the Internet, while Bangladeshi farmers can learn about pest management techniques through the World Wide Web.

In so far as globalization is the result of technological progress, efforts to slow or reverse it are futile and reactionary. Those who try to obstruct globalization today are caught up in the same naive and futile project that was undertaken by the English Luddites during the early days of the Industrial Revolution. The Luddites convinced themselves that they could frustrate industrialization and thereby protect their jobs and idealized rural communities by sabotaging machines.

Efforts to curtail globalization suffer from misplaced fears and self-interest. But to the degree that they are successful, these efforts to stall globalization necessarily reduce global living standards by preventing a more efficient allocation of resources. Even worse, anti-globalization strategies in high-income countries retard growth and perpetuate poverty in the developing world.

> Globalization makes it extremely costly, if not impossible, for countries to maintain anything but market-friendly, neoliberal economic policies.

The pressures and opportunities associated with globalization provide incentives for governments to pursue the 'right policies'

– that is, neoliberal economic policies (see Chapters 2 and 6). This argument is straightforward: the benefits of globalization are available only to countries that permit the free, market-mediated flow of goods and capital. Countries that restrict imports deprive themselves of the opportunity to purchase goods produced elsewhere in the world at attractive prices. This harms consumers, and undermines export performance by forcing domestic producers to utilize more costly domestic inputs in the production process. Moreover, countries that restrict investor or business freedoms (through tariffs, capital controls, excessive government regulations, etc.) will be pariahs in international financial markets. Investors will demand a premium on their funds to invest in such inhospitable countries, and these higher capital costs will cripple economic growth. Investors also shun countries that have lax fiscal or monetary management. This means that countries that seek to attract foreign investment must maintain a sound macroeconomic environment.

The choice, then, is clear. Globalization and neoliberal economic policies (hereafter 'neoliberal globalization') are essential to the promotion of high living standards and prosperity. While the transition to open markets and policy discipline may generate short-term pain (such as a temporary rise in unemployment), the long-term benefits of these strategies are immense. It is therefore unsurprising that policymakers in nearly all countries (save North Korea and a few others) have come to embrace these keys to prosperity.

3.3 **The Myth Rejected**

> Globalization is not the inevitable outcome of technological advances.

Historical evidence does not support the claim that advances in transportation and communications technologies necessarily induce globalization. These technologies have progressed almost continuously over the last two centuries, but the progress of globalization during this time has been highly uneven. For example, levels of economic globalization – measured in a variety of ways – were considerably higher in the late nineteenth century, when international commerce depended on steamships and telegraphs, than they were in the 1950s, 1960s and 1970s, when transportation and communications technologies were much further advanced.[2]

> Political decisions – rather than technology – are the primary driving force behind the pace and form of globalization. Technology merely defines the realm of possibilities.

The pace and form of globalization that prevail at any point in time are the result of deliberate policy choices. Thus the neoliberal globalization of the last two decades stems directly from government initiatives in industrialized and developing countries from the late 1970s and early 1980s, respectively. International institutions, such as the IMF and the WTO, have also played a critically important role in promoting policies that facilitate the rapid pace and neoliberal character of globalization in most developing countries today.

To be sure, technology is not a trivial player in the globalization process. Technology delimits what is possible, such as how quickly and under what conditions goods and finance can flow across national borders. But whether these flows will be permitted depends on political decisions in the realm of international trade and financial policy. For instance, since the 1980s the extent of international financial speculation has intensified dramatically. This development is not due to the advent of the Internet, as the technologies necessary for rapid flows of speculative finance (such as the telephone and the fax machine) existed prior to the 1980s. Speculation has become more prevalent because opportunities and incentives to speculate have been created by policies of financial liberalization.

The link between globalization and neoliberalism can be broken.

While being critical of the neoliberal discourse on globalization, we also reject the claim that globalization itself is at the heart of many of the economic and social problems observed in developing countries. *It is the neoliberal form of globalization that is being promoted so aggressively today — and not globalization itself — that is chiefly responsible for the poor economic performance and the deterioration of living standards in so many countries* (see Chapter 2).

Neoliberals maintain that success in a globalized world economy depends on the creation of a neoliberal policy environment on the domestic and international levels. Indeed, they claim that eventually all countries will converge around this policy regime, since any other regime will be severely punished by global markets.

These arguments are simply incorrect. Globalization is perfectly compatible with different degrees and patterns of openness (to trade and capital flows) at the national level. The 1950s and 1960s combined rapid globalization with extensive economic regulation, in developing and industrialized countries alike. Thus globalization and neoliberalism are not necessarily two sides of the same coin.

The argument that the competitive pressures fostered by globalization make it necessary for all countries to converge to the same neoliberal economic model is not borne out by evidence (as we will see in Chapters 5, 7–11; see also Berger and Dore 1996). A considerable degree of policy and institutional diversity exists among industrialized countries today, despite the progress of globalization. For example, Sweden, Austria, the Netherlands, France and Germany have all maintained policies and institutional arrangements that are quite distinct from those in the neoliberal economies of the USA and the UK. Larger and/or richer developing countries — especially China, India, Taiwan and Malaysia — have also managed to maintain non-neoliberal policy regimes. To be sure, smaller and/or poorer developing countries confront more severe restrictions on their policy autonomy. But even these countries may enjoy greater policy autonomy than is generally recognized. Chile is an example of a developing country that pursued a generally neoliberal path in the 1990s, but nevertheless managed to maintain a rather stringent regime of capital controls (see Chapter 9).

In sum, the neoliberal globalization that has been emerging over the past several decades is but one form of globalization. *Different policy choices (particularly as concern trade and financial policies) can create a form of globalization that would not be so noxious to living standards and growth prospects in developing countries.* Numerous examples of such policy alternatives are provided in Part II of this book.

Notes

1. Regular transatlantic steamship service was inaugurated in 1838, but until the 1860s the ships mainly carried high-value goods (as do airplanes today). Steamships started to dominate sailing ships only from the 1870s (O'Rourke and Williamson 1999: 33–4). The first telegraph system was patented in 1837. The first successful long-distance telegraph transmission was made in the USA in 1844. The first successful transatlantic telegraph cable was laid in 1868 (Held et al. 1999: 335).

2. There are many measures of globalization. Frequently used measures include international trade or short-term international capital flows as a percentage of a nation's total economic activity, and the share of immigrants in total population.

'The neoliberal American model of
capitalism represents the ideal that all
developing countries should seek to
replicate'

4.1   **The Myth**

By now it is clear that American neoliberalism has outperformed
all other economic systems. Any lingering doubts about this matter were erased during the 1990s when the USA prospered while
other economies faltered. The demise of these systems exposes
the failure of all forms of 'statism' and heralds the inevitable
convergence of all nations upon the American model that em-
braces neoliberalism and democracy.

4.2   **The Myth Explored**

The 'new economy' of the 1990s reflects the dynamism and
superiority of the US economic model.

During the 1990s the US economy experienced sustained economic
and productivity growth, low unemployment and low inflation. The
2001 *Economic Report of the* [US] *President* (ERP: ch. 1) reports that
from the first quarter of 1993 through the third quarter of 2000
real GDP grew at an average annual rate of 4 per cent – which
was 46 per cent faster than the average rate from 1973 to 1993;
productivity (i.e. output created per hour of work) of non-farm
jobs grew at an average rate of 2.3 per cent per year, compared
to an average of 1.4 per cent per year for the previous twenty
years; the number of jobs increased by more than 22 million while

the unemployment rate declined steadily (reaching 3.9 per cent in 2000, the lowest level in a generation); and core inflation (i.e. the rate of inflation excluding price increases in food and energy) remained at a tolerable 2–3 per cent. These achievements are evidence of a 'new economy' that was fuelled by the information and telecommunications technology revolution. It may even be that this new economy is not susceptible to the business cycles that had plagued capitalist development for centuries.

The USA was the natural launching pad for the new economy, given its innovation-promoting regulatory regime and the prevalence of market incentives. For example, intellectual property rights (IPRs) are well protected, business taxes are low, employee compensation is based on performance (rather than on seniority or favouritism), business transparency is promoted by the legal environment, and the government does not discourage private initiative through excessive expenditure.

While the 'old' mass production economy of the USA clearly stumbled in the 1970s and 1980s, the country has demonstrated that its flexible, competitive and privatized economic system is uniquely capable of generating new technologies and new forms of commerce. This type of dynamism and adaptability is the recipe for success in a world economy that is now characterized by globalization and driven by rapid technological progress (see also Chapters 1–3).

The uncertainties in the global political and economic environment that have followed the events of 11 September 2001 have taken a toll on the US economy, of course. But there is no cause for fundamental concern. History has proven the inherent resilience of the US economy. Indeed, the flexibility of the US economy has enabled it to emerge from any difficulties more quickly than the rigid and inefficient economies of Europe and Japan.

> The superiority of the US model is also evidenced by the
> failings of the economies of Continental Europe and Japan.

The recent experiences of Continental Europe and Japan confirm the desirability of American neoliberalism. The interventionist economies of Continental Europe have been plagued by slow growth and high unemployment since the 1980s. Fortunately, many of the region's economies have recently begun to undertake bold, American-style economic reform. European nations have begun to deregulate and privatize industry, open up to trade, capital and labour flows within the region, and pursue monetary discipline under the leadership of the new European Central Bank. As a consequence they have begun to show modest signs of economic recovery (with regard to improved investor confidence, growth, etc.).

In contrast, Japan's situation remains dire. The country has been stalled in recession for over a decade, a consequence of its overregulated economy. Unfortunately, Japanese policymakers appear unwilling to develop a plan to restore economic prosperity through radical deregulation.

The superiority of American neoliberalism is also demonstrated by the enviable performance of those countries that have patterned their economies on that of the USA, namely the 'Anglo-American economies' of the UK, Canada, New Zealand and Australia. All have performed impressively during the 1990s.

In sum, the record is clear: the neoliberal American model of capitalism outperforms all other economic models. It is uniquely positioned to respond to new technological challenges and to deliver growth and prosperity in today's world economy. Though the anti-market economic systems of Europe and East Asia never constituted an ideal, the present juncture finds them positively outdated (see also Chapter 5).

4.3 **The Myth Rejected**

American triumphalism is based on wishful thinking rather than on a careful, objective analysis.

There are several reasons to reject claims for the superiority of US capitalism, particularly in relation to its performance in the 1990s. The case for exporting this model to the developing world is, in a word, underwhelming.

There never was a new economy in the 1990s.[1]

Contrary to the claims of new economy enthusiasts, US economic performance during the 1990s was rather unimpressive. In fact, the US grew more slowly in the 'new-economy' 1990s than in the preceding periods. Focusing on the first several years of business upturns in successive decades, economist Dean Baker finds that the average growth rate of GDP from 1991 to 1995 was 2.7 per cent, while growth averaged 4.4 per cent from 1982 to 1986 and 4.8 per cent from 1970 to 1973 (Baker 2000). US economic growth was notable only during 1996–99 (as GDP growth averaged 4 per cent over the four years from 1995 to 1999). But these few years of strong growth in the latter portion of the 1990s only offset the anaemic growth of the preceding period. Moreover, Baker argues that the impressive growth in the late 1990s is partly an illusion stemming from a change in US government measurement techniques.

A similar story can be told of US productivity growth. The average annual rate of productivity growth was 1.9 per cent during the 1990s, compared to an average annual rate of close to 3 per cent in the twenty-five years that followed World War II and 1.4 per cent for the years 1973 to 1989. As with economic growth, productivity growth was only strong during the later years of the 1990s: productivity growth averaged 2.5 per cent from 1995 to 1999; and some of the apparent increase in productivity growth is attributable to changes in measurement. Baker's analysis of US performance during the 1990s concludes that claims for a new economy are empirically unsupported.

The 1990s boom did not benefit the lives of ordinary Americans.

US economic performance during the 1990s also looks quite different when one takes account of distributional issues (see also Chapter 2). The US stock market boom of the 1990s – itself a consequence of the new economy hype – redounded to the benefit of the wealthiest 20 per cent (and especially the wealthiest 1 per cent) of the population, and provided only meagre benefits to the average American family (Wolff 2000). Similarly, the increasing inequality in US wages that began in the 1980s continued through the 1990s, as wage increases went disproportionately to the most affluent (Baker 2000).[2]

The economic boom of the 1990s did little to eradicate poverty.[3] Indeed, the US Census Bureau reported in June 2002 that the proportion of families classified as poor remained virtually unchanged between 1989 and 2000 (*New York Times*, 5 June 2002). In 2000, 9.2 per cent of US families were classified as poor, compared to 10 per cent in 1989.

> The collapse of the US stock market bubble of the 1990s reveals a disturbing pattern of corporate corruption and resource misallocation.

Throughout the 1990s, economists lauded the incentives associated with the US system of executive compensation as a spur to efficiency and rapid innovation. Corporate executives garnered extremely high salaries, stock options (which gave them the right, but not the obligation, to buy or sell stocks by a future date at an agreed-upon price) and other perks.

These compensation packages resulted in vast disparities between the compensation of executives and average workers within the same firm. For example, in 1970 the average inflation-adjusted annual compensation of the top one hundred chief executive officers (CEOs) in the USA was $1.3 million – 39 times the pay of an average worker. By 1999, the average compensation of the top one hundred CEOs had risen to $37.5 million, more than 1,000 times the pay of an average worker (Krugman 2002: 64).

These executive compensation packages represented a massive misallocation of resources as firms were managed with the objective of maximizing the short-term value of the stock options held by highly placed insiders (see Chapters 8.1 and 10). The financial and corporate environment of the 1990s also promoted myriad forms of corruption. The US corporate corruption and accounting scandals of 2002 revealed that many corporate executives, boards and external auditors were seduced by the huge rewards available through stock appreciation. They manipulated accounting and other information to fuel an unsustainable rise in stock prices.

> Many other industrialized countries performed at least as well as the USA and other Anglo-American economies during the 1990s.

US economic performance during the 1990s also fails to impress when one considers it in comparative perspective. Many other industrialized countries performed as well or better than the USA during the 1990s. For example, between 1990 and 2000, Ireland (with a growth rate of 6.8 per cent), Singapore (5.3 per cent), Norway (3.1 per cent), Australia (2.8 per cent), Portugal (2.6 per cent) and Finland (2.4 per cent) grew at least as fast as the USA, while many others, such as Denmark (2.3 per cent), the Netherlands (2.2 per cent), Spain (2.2 per cent) and the UK (2.2 per cent), grew almost as fast.

As a group, the Anglo-American economies did not fare terribly well during the 1990s. New Zealand and the UK were at the forefront of neoliberal reform during the last two decades. But these reforms seem to have had no discernible effect on their economic performance. Indeed, economic growth rates in the USA, UK and New Zealand were nearly identical during the neoliberal era of 1980–2000 and the interventionist era of 1960–79 (see also Chapter 2). The neoliberal era did, however, bring with it a striking increase in inequality within these nations.

Notes

1. The data in this and the following paragraph are taken from Baker 2000.
2. US wage gains during the 1990s were quite modest. Baker (2002) reports that real hourly wages for typical US workers rose at an annual rate of 0.5 per cent from June 1990 to March 2001. Although

real hourly wages rose at an annual rate of 1.5 per cent from 1995 to 2001, they fell at an average rate of 0.4 per cent annually from 1990 to 1995.

3. Reform of the social welfare system in the USA (involving significant curtailment of transfer payments to the poor) also contributed to the stagnation in poverty levels in the 1990s.

5 **Myth 5**

'The East Asian model is idiosyncratic;
the Anglo-American model is universal'

5.1 **The Myth**

Contrary to the conventional wisdom of the 1980s, the East Asian economic model is not replicable elsewhere. In contrast, the Anglo-American model is universally applicable. Policymakers in developing countries must therefore accept the Anglo-American economic model as the only path to prosperity (see also Chapter 4).

5.2 **The Myth Explored**

The East Asian model cannot work outside of the region as its success depends on unique historical, political and cultural conditions.

The East Asian model departed quite radically from what we know to be the 'best practices' associated with the neoliberal, Anglo-American model. For several decades, the model flourished: it generated historically unprecedented increases in the rate of economic growth, improvements in living standards, and economic modernization.

These achievements hardly imply that the East Asian model should or even can be transplanted to other parts of the developing world, however. Indeed, the East Asian financial crisis of 1997 and the persistence of economic stagnation in Japan are evidence of the model's failings. Most importantly, the East Asian model depends on a number of conditions that cannot be replicated elsewhere.

There are five unique characteristics of East Asian countries that were pivotal to the success of this model.

First, the East Asian countries share a common Confucian culture. This cultural heritage helps to explain the pronounced work ethic, the devotion to saving, the commitment to invest in education, and the willingness to obey authoritarian governments. Absent this cultural heritage, it is very difficult to imagine any country being able to accumulate physical and human capital as quickly as did the East Asian countries. The authoritarian tradition in East Asia also made it possible to pursue industrial policies that were highly centralized and to maintain repressive labour policies. Finally, Confucian culture bequeathed highly developed state bureaucracies, which were necessary to the success of their complex trade and industrial policies.

Second, East Asian countries are far more ethnically homogeneous than most other developing countries. Ethnic homogeneity makes it far easier to build consensus and implement policy.

Third, East Asian countries are blessed with poor resource endowments, and were therefore able to avoid what some call the 'resource curse'. Plentiful resources tend to dampen competitive pressures and to induce wasteful political struggles over the control of such resources. Unlike many resource-rich countries in Latin America and Africa, the East Asian countries were forced to work hard and to create wealth through manufacturing.

Fourth, East Asian countries benefited in vital ways from Japanese colonialism. Unlike its Western counterpart, Japanese colonialism left behind a strong industrial base, an educated population, and an advanced infrastructure.

Last not but least, the East Asian model benefited from propitious external circumstances. The Cold War allowed Japan and other 'frontier states' against Communism to prosper under the umbrella of US defence spending and economic aid. East Asian countries also benefited from a 'permissive' international political environment up until the 1980s that allowed them to engage in mercantilist trade policies (e.g. subsidizing exports) and even to cheat their way to prosperity by violating the trademarks and patents held by industrialized countries. In contrast, today's WTO rules regarding subsidies and IPRs preclude developing countries from adopting key aspects of the East Asian model.

In sum, the success of the East Asian model depended on this unique set of internal and external conditions. This fortuitous combination of circumstances cannot be replicated elsewhere.

> The Anglo-American model is consistent with universal human values.

Unlike the East Asian model, the Anglo-American model is consistent with universal aspects of human nature: namely, the natural tendency for entrepreneurship, the desire for wealth, and the driving force of self-interest. The Anglo-American model is therefore appropriate to and can succeed in all societies. It is no coincidence that so many countries are rushing to adopt this model these days.

5.3 **The Myth Rejected**

> The achievements of the East Asian economic model are not explained by the region's special conditions.

Arguments that emphasize the role of unique internal and external circumstances in the success of the East Asian model range from exaggerated to incorrect. We consider these arguments in turn.

Confucianism is now seen as a kind of magical culture that fosters the development of a competent corps of civil servants, high levels of savings and educational investment, and a pliant population. This new view of Confucianism differs markedly from the view that predominated until the 1950s. The latter presented the culture as inimical to economic development. For example, at the time it was widely argued that the old Confucian social hierarchy, a hierarchy that placed bureaucrats at the top of the social order and artisans and merchants at the bottom, induced talented people to choose bureaucratic over business or engineering careers.

Despite this view of Confucianism, civil servants in Korea and Taiwan were widely regarded as highly inadequate in the 1950s and 1960s. By that time, the early Confucian tradition of meritocracy and competitive recruitment practices had decayed. In fact, the civil service corps had deteriorated so greatly in Korea that until the 1960s the country was sending its public servants to Pakistan and the Philippines for training. Hence, the early success with the East Asian model (at least in some countries) did not depend on the presence of an extraordinarily competent public sector. Later on these countries did, in fact, benefit from a high level of public-sector competency. But this competency (for example, in Korea and Taiwan) was created through the expenditure of substantial political energy and economic resources. It was not a legacy of the country's history or culture.

The claim that ethnic homogeneity played an important role in the success of the East Asian model is exaggerated. Singapore is, in fact, a multi-ethnic society. In Taiwan there has been a rather strong tension between two major 'ethnic' groups – the 'Taiwanese', the descendants of the immigrants from Southeast China since the sixteenth century, and the 'Mainlanders', those who moved with the Nationalist government after its defeat by the Communists in 1949. Finally, while it is true that Korea has one of the most homogeneous populations in the world, this does not imply that efforts to build national consensus on key issues has been easy. There are intense regional rivalries within the country. These rivalries render efforts to build genuine national consensus extremely difficult.

The claim that East Asia benefited from the scarcity of its natural resource base is unpersuasive. A rich endowment of natural resources can certainly create perverse political and economic dynamics. But this hardly implies that countries are better off if they are resource poor. During the late nineteenth and early twentieth centuries the fastest growing economies in the world had abundant natural resources. Among these were countries in North and South America, Oceania (Australia and New Zealand) and Scandinavia.

The claim that East Asian countries emerged from Japanese colonialism in a far better position than did countries colonized by Western powers is misleading. For example, Korea's literacy ratio at the end of Japanese colonialism in 1945 was only 22 per cent. This literacy ratio was not much better than that of many African countries when they emerged from colonialism. By contrast, Argentina's literacy ratio in 1945 was over 90 per cent. More generally, there were at least a dozen African countries whose post-colonial conditions were equal or even superior to those of Korea.

On the matter of a propitious external environment, it is certainly true that Cold War politics brought large pools of aid from the USA to Korea and Taiwan in the 1950s. However, by the 1960s these levels of aid fell significantly, and on average were not much greater than the levels of aid that went to many developing countries. During the 1960s and the 1970s, Chile and the Philippines, for instance, received US aid packages that were as generous as those given to Korea and Taiwan, but with much less effect. Also, the economic benefits of Cold War-related aid must be balanced against the costs of being a frontier state against Communism. As frontier states, Korea and Taiwan maintained high levels of defence spending (equivalent to about 6 per cent or more of national income, compared to the world average of 2–3 per cent[1]) and had a significant proportion of their able-bodied young workers in the military service for three years or longer. It is also estimated that the Korean War (1950–53) destroyed more than half of the country's manufacturing base and more than three-quarters of the rail system and other infrastructure.

It is true that East Asian economies benefited from a more permissive international environment regarding trade protection and IPRs. Certainly, the WTO now precludes many of the practices associated with the East Asian model. But, having said this, one must not view the predecessor of the WTO, the GATT, too lightly. Many of the strategies pursued in East Asia were also disallowed under the GATT. The East Asian countries exercised a good deal of policy creativity in their successful efforts to exploit loopholes and grey areas in the GATT.[2] Opportunities to exploit ambiguities in the WTO exist today as well (see Chapter 7 and Chapter 8.2). That said, developing countries should press the WTO and other multilaterals for the latitude to engage in the kinds of non-neoliberal strategies that today's industrialized countries used so effectively in the past.

> Empirically, the East Asian model has played a far more important role in promoting economic development around the world than has the Anglo-American model.

An honest examination of the historical record reveals that most of today's industrialized countries utilized an economic model that was far closer to the East Asian model than it was to the Anglo-American model (see Chapters 1, 7–11). Thus it seems that the East Asian model (in all of its national variants) is closer to a world norm than is the Anglo-American model. The experiences of the USA and the UK are particularly notable: during their own development these countries maintained policies towards trade, industry and IPRs that were akin to those used later in East Asia (see Chapters 1 and 7, and Chapter 8.2).

> The specious special conditions argument could just as easily be invoked to explain the economic success of the USA and UK.

Though we find the special conditions line of reasoning highly problematic, it can just as easily be applied to explain US and UK development as East Asian development. Britain, for example, prospered at a time in history when it could (and did) colonize and/or dominate weaker nations, engage in slave trade, openly sell opium to China, and force young children to work 12-hour days under miserable working conditions. During its development, Britain also routinely violated IPRs (see Chapter 8.2) and maintained a law from 1750 to 1842 that banned exports of machinery to competitor economies. The economy of the USA benefited from very similar circumstances. Additionally, the USA benefited from its vast geographic scope (as the government was able to exterminate and/or forcibly relocate Native Americans), a large population of immigrant labour, and its exceptionally rich endowment of natural resources.

The USA and Britain clearly benefited from many circumstances that are not available to developing countries today. Neoliberals are therefore wrong to hold the Anglo-American countries as a model for developing countries today since their unique attributes and experiences cannot be replicated (see Chapter 4). More generally, every country is unique with regard to its mix of history, culture, ethnic composition, the timing of its development, and so on. Thus the experience of East Asian countries is no more or no less idiosyncratic than is the experience of any other country. *Our goal in this book is to examine the wide range of policies that have enabled and can promote economic development without making claims for the universality of any one path* (see Chapters 7–11).

The Anglo-American model is not universal.

Though neoliberals frequently claim otherwise, there is no evidence of any universal, intrinsic human drive towards commerce, individualism or the accretion of wealth. In our view, then, the success of the Anglo-American model is grounded in something far less universal: it depends on a host of specific institutional and regulatory preconditions (see Chapters 4, 8.2 and 10). Absent these prerequisites, the Anglo-American model cannot function properly.

Evidence for this view comes from all parts of the globe during the 1980s and 1990s, as countries have struggled to install the Anglo-American model. The numerous failures of these efforts (especially in the former Soviet republics) underscore the difficulty of this project, even were it to be desirable. In their zeal to export the Anglo-American model, neoliberals often overlook the fact that the creation of its institutional prerequisites (e.g. a developed system of financial regulation) requires a significant expenditure of human and financial resources and also takes a good deal of time. Moreover, even with the necessary resources and time, there may well be aspects of the necessary institutional and regulatory foundation that are not compatible with the existing political, cultural and institutional characteristics of particular developing countries.

Notes

1. The average military spending for the IMF's 130 member countries was 3.6 per cent of GDP in 1990 and 2.4 per cent of GDP in 1995 (Clements et al. 1996).
2. Note that Taiwan was not a member of the GATT for political reasons.

6 **Myth 6**

'Developing countries need the discipline
provided by international institutions
and by politically independent domestic
policymaking institutions'

6.1 **The Myth**

Politicians and government employees are untrustworthy. They
typically manipulate the policy tools and resources at their disposal to maintain or expand their power rather than work for
the interests of the broader society. The only way to ensure
government accountability is to create an institutional structure
that keeps these tendencies in check and/or rewards appropriate
behaviour.

6.2 **The Myth Explored**

> Economic policy should not be left in the hands of politicians
> and government officials.

During the 1980s, the consensus view regarding the public sector
changed dramatically. Previously, politicians and government employees were largely seen as working for the public good, and consequently were commonly referred to as 'public servants'. But during
the 1980s, thanks to the neoliberal intellectual revolution, people
finally began to see politicians and government officials as what
they really are – self-interested (and sometimes corrupt) agents
promoting their own agenda, rather than the public good.

The chief problem with the public sector is that it lacks the institutional incentives to ensure that the self-interested behaviour of officials serves the broader social good. By contrast, the market mechanism in the private sector serves the critical function of aligning self-interest and the social good.

The failure of the public sector is most severe and consequential in developing countries. In industrialized countries, public officials are held accountable (to an extent) by democratic political systems, the free press, legal systems, transparent rules and strong anti-corruption measures. But these mechanisms are often absent in the developing world. Here we find underdeveloped democratic and legal processes, opaque rules, press censorship, weak (or non-existent) anti-corruption measures and incompetence. This context breeds government corruption and inefficiency that undermine economic development initiatives.

> The record shows that the discipline associated with politically independent economic institutions is absolutely essential in developing countries.

Given this context, it is vitally necessary to place policymaking authority in the hands of the technocrats that staff powerful, politically independent policymaking institutions, such as central banks and currency boards (see Chapter 11). These measures promote efficiency while enhancing the confidence of foreign and domestic investors.

Unfortunately, creating politically independent policymaking institutions at the national level often fails to ensure rational economic policymaking. Government officials often find ways to interfere in the decisions of even nominally independent domestic policymaking institutions, particularly during economic downturns or when elections approach. Developing countries also often lack a sufficient cadre of competent local economists to staff independent domestic policymaking institutions.

In view of these difficulties, international institutions, such as the IMF, the World Bank and the WTO, can greatly enhance the integrity and quality of economic policy in developing countries. Countries that submit to their authority import appropriate policy and win the confidence of domestic and foreign investors. Sadly, reactionary left- and right-wing critics of international institutions typically overstate the degree to which they abridge national sovereignty, and fail to appreciate the universal nature of the policies that these institutions promote. Critics also often fail to acknowledge the role these institutions play in filling an 'expertise gap' in developing countries that lack a sufficient corps of skilled economists and the resources necessary for them to work effectively.

In short, independent domestic and international policymaking institutions ensure that governments pursue economic policies that promote long-term economic development, prosperity and the universal social good.

6.3 **The Myth Rejected**

> Public officials have designed good economic policy in a great many countries.

The rhetoric of neoliberalism generated, rather than revealed, a virulent distrust and denigration of government and of public officials. But this view of the public sector and public officials sits rather uneasily with the historical record. In many countries, the public sector and public institutions have played an essential, positive role in the development process.

> There is no evidence that public officials are inherently corrupt or undermine the policymaking process.

Public officials are not inherently more corrupt, ambitious of position, or less efficient than are their counterparts in the private sector (see Chapters 7–11). Nor does the private sector do a better job of preventing socially harmful behaviour. Corruption scandals occur with equal frequency in the public and private sectors. This is even the case in a country like the USA, where the private sector is seen as an exemplar of sound business practices and where regulatory bodies are supposed to be vigilant monitors against malfeasance by the private sector. The numerous corporate corruption scandals of 2002 (e.g. Enron, Arthur Andersen) are just the latest examples of a long history of private-sector corruption in the USA. The problems of collusion, bribery and the tendency towards business concentration and monopolization represent private-sector analogues to the self-aggrandizing actions of some public officials.

The association between the private sector and efficiency (and the public sector and inefficiency) is fanciful. Large private-sector firms can be vast, slow-moving bureaucracies that create innumerable opportunities for self-aggrandizement, ruinous rivalries, cheating and waste. Moreover, 'efficiency' is a complex (and contentious) term. Not least, there are many different types of efficiency – efficiency with regard to responding to changes in market conditions, efficiency with regard to meeting certain social objectives (such as eliminating poverty) and so forth – and it is by no means clear that an institution that is efficient in any one sense will be equally (or at all) efficient in others. Finally, whether or not the private or the public sector functions with integrity and/or efficiency depends very much on the capacities, compensation, incentives and standing of actors in these positions, on the regulatory and institutional climate in which they operate, and on the broader political and juridical context in which their jobs are performed.

> Placing policymaking authority in the hands of unelected technocrats runs counter to principles of democracy, accountability and transparency. Moreover, this strategy does not even improve long-term economic performance.

By generating distrust and disregard for the public sector, neo-liberalism provides a rationale for the necessity of transferring policymaking authority to the technocrats that staff politically independent institutions. In this scheme, then, monetary policy is delegated to independent central banks, exchange rate policy is delegated to currency boards, and fiscal policy is delegated to fiscal boards (see Chapter 11). Regulatory authority over public utilities is increasingly being delegated to independent 'expert agencies'. At the same time, international institutions and rules are playing an increasingly important role in defining the scope of acceptable domestic economic policies. The IMF is quite influential when it comes to policy oversight and the establishment of firm guidelines (and even strictures) for economic policy in developing countries. This is particularly the case in the context of economic crises. Additionally, domestic economic regulations and policies are increasingly subject to international rules established by the WTO (see Chapters 7 and 8.2).

The delegation of policymaking authority to independent domestic and/or international bodies is highly objectionable. This strategy denies the value of democratic governance and obscures the policy process from public view. Politically independent institutions are by definition not accountable to the public and tend to serve the interests of the narrow constituencies with which they are closely associated. For example, the IMF and the World Bank are accountable to the global financial community and to the powerful governments that dominate their agenda. Independent central banks and currency boards take their cues from the financial community. Powerful, wealthy countries and business interests exercise disproportionate influence over the WTO.

From the neoliberal perspective, one of the key advantages of politically independent policymaking institutions is that their mission cannot be corrupted by popular demands. But the neoliberal argument flies in the face of the neoliberal emphasis on freedom in the economic domain, where people are presumed to be entirely rational and in possession of sufficient economic knowledge, wisdom and judgement to know what is in their best interest. It dismisses the principle of self-governance, in favour of governance by an elite cadre of neoliberal economists.

As we will see in Part II (Chapters 7, 8.2 and 11.1–11.2), delegating policy to independent authorities is also economically undesirable. To date, there is no evidence that insulating policy from the political process improves economic performance in any significant respect. But there is overwhelming evidence that this strategy imposes severe costs on the economy and, especially, on the most vulnerable segments of society. This finding contradicts the neoliberal view that independent policymaking institutions are neutral guardians of the national interest. These institutions typically meet the needs of investors, lenders and business interests rather than serve the public good (see also Chapter 2).

Part II

Economic Policy Alternatives

Part II is a manual of economic policy. It is intended for present and aspiring policymakers in developing countries, for those working in nongovernmental and multilateral organizations, and for students of development policy. Each chapter presents a thorough analysis of specific areas of economic policy. Our discussion of policy is not exhaustive. It does, however, focus on those policy domains where new thinking is most urgently needed, and where there exist sound and feasible alternatives to the neoliberal policies that have been promoted so forcefully over the last two decades.

The discussion of each policy area has three components. First, we present the arguments advanced by neoliberals for a particular economic policy ('The neoliberal view'). Here we present the best case for the neoliberal view, and the economic logic that underpins it. Where necessary, we demystify the technical jargon that often prevents non-economists from grasping the arguments advanced by neoliberals. Second, we present a series of counterarguments to the neoliberal case for the policy in question ('Rejection of the neoliberal view'). We refute the case advanced by neoliberals by drawing on economic logic and empirical, cross-country and/or historical evidence. Third, we discuss a range of policies that, in our view, are economically desirable and feasible alternatives to those advanced by neoliberal economists in a specific policy domain ('Policy alternatives'). Readers may wish to consult the 'Recommended Further Reading' section for references to work by neoliberal economists and by those advancing alternative views in particular policy areas.

7 **Policy Alternatives I**

Trade and Industry

7.1 **Trade Policy**

The neoliberal view

The best trade policy is that of free trade.

Free trade refers to trade that is unimpeded by tariffs or other types of government restriction. Put simply, free trade is the ideal to which all developing countries (indeed, all countries) should strive. Free trade carries numerous benefits. It offers developing countries the opportunity to attain higher rates of output and employment growth, to increase productivity and efficiency, and to enhance living standards and consumption choices. Free trade also corrodes corrupt systems of preference wherein those with connections to the government are granted trade licences and other protections.

The case for free trade is based on the universally accepted theory of comparative advantage.

The theory of comparative advantage holds that if the government does not 'distort' trade, a country will specialize in the production and export of those goods for which it is best suited, given its endowments of land, labour and capital. A country has a comparative advantage in an industry if its relative performance in that industry (i.e. its performance as compared with other countries) is better than its relative performance in other industries. This implies that every country will have a comparative advantage in something. Even a country that is relatively inefficient in all industries when compared with other countries – in which it does not have what is called an 'absolute advantage' in any industry – will nevertheless have a comparative advantage in that industry where its performance is least deficient.

An example might help to clarify. Let us assume that China and Germany both produce stuffed toys and automobiles. Assume further that Germany is more efficient than China in both industries – it therefore enjoys an absolute advantage in both. But if the gap between the two countries is smaller in toy manufacture – if China's deficiency is least in this industry – then we say that China has a comparative advantage in toys, while Germany has a comparative advantage in automobiles.

How does this bear on the matter of trade? Trade theory contends that under free trade each country can and will specialize in that industry where it has a comparative advantage, and will trade with its partner to secure that good for which it does not. In our case, China will export toys in exchange for automobiles. With each country specializing in this way, trade theory demonstrates that each country will become better off than it was prior to trade, when each was forced to produce some of both goods.

Thus seen, the theory of comparative advantage has heartening implications for developing countries since many of them do not have an absolute cost advantage in the production of any single product. But there is always some product that can be produced *relatively less inefficiently*. Free trade, then, allows each country to obtain from other countries those goods that are not produced domestically.

The theory of comparative advantage also provides a basis for rejecting state intervention in production and trade. Government intervention in production or trade distorts price signals regarding the relative profitability associated with the production of different products, given existing resources. This distortion can lead a country to specialize in the production of a product for which it does not have a comparative advantage. As a result, the country will produce fewer total products and social welfare will suffer accordingly.

Revisiting the China–Germany example illuminates this argument. Say that the Chinese government protects its nascent automobile industry from competition with Germany by imposing a tariff on German auto imports. If this tariff is sufficiently high, Chinese consumers will not purchase German autos and will instead purchase autos produced in China. The increase in demand for Chinese autos will cause Chinese entrepreneurs to exit other lines of business (such as toy production) and enter the auto industry. But this switch in product specialization will not benefit the Chinese economy as a whole. This is because the country's resources make it relatively less efficient at auto as compared to toy production. The total output of China will therefore suffer as a direct result of the decision to encourage auto production.

> The theory of comparative advantage also provides a rationale for unilateral trade liberalization.

In global fora (such as the World Trade Organization), developing countries frequently complain that industrialized countries are not open to their exports. However, the theory of comparative advantage can be invoked to demonstrate that developing countries are better off rescinding trade barriers regardless of what their trading partners do. The policies of a country's trade partners are thus irrelevant.

We illustrate this point by returning again to the China–Germany example. Even if Germany imposes tariffs on toy imports from China, China will nevertheless benefit by removing its tariffs on German automobiles. As it does so, Chinese consumers will enjoy a higher standard of living, since they now can secure automobiles more cheaply. The German tariffs on Chinese toys will principally harm German consumers, who must pay higher prices than necessary for this item.

> The historical and statistical record demonstrates that free trade is critical to development.

Today's industrialized countries developed on the basis of free trade (see also Chapter 1). The economies of the USA and the UK, in particular, demonstrate the benefits of free trade, though almost all industrialized countries embraced free trade during their development. There is also ample statistical evidence to buttress the case for free trade. These studies show that countries with less restricted trade have grown faster than their counterparts in the post-World War II era.[1]

> There are some legitimate public policy rationales for certain tariffs, but these rationales are highly limited.

Governments in developing countries may sometimes resort to tariffs as a way to raise revenue or to provide temporary protection to new industries that are of national importance. If governments do impose tariffs (though other options should be explored first), it is essential that they are low and uniform across products. Uniform tariffs mean that each imported product is taxed at the same rate. Low, uniform tariffs will minimize distortions because they do not encourage domestic producers to move into the production of any single product line. It is generally agreed that uniform tariff rates on imports should be kept at around 5 per cent.

There may also be reasons to protect some new domestic industries from international competition. However, this type of protection, termed infant industry protection, must be temporary (i.e. in place for no more than 5–8 years) and should only be pursued if the industry has a strong chance of success. The tariff used to protect infant industries should be in the range of 5–10 per cent, and should not exceed 20 per cent under any circumstances.[2] Note that revenue and infant-industry tariffs are permissible by the WTO so long as they stay roughly within the provisos mentioned here.

> Since the 1980s, governments in many developing countries have vigorously pursued trade liberalization because they have finally begun to appreciate its virtues.

The recent move to freer (if not totally free) trade by many developing countries shows that their governments have finally acknowledged the failure of programmes to protect inefficient domestic industries in the name of import-substituting industrialization (ISI). The debt crisis of the 1980s promoted radical trade liberalization in developing countries. This is because trade liberalization was a key component of the structural adjustment programmes (SAPs) of the IMF/World Bank. In many cases, the trade liberalization component of SAPs provided governments with political cover for the otherwise difficult task of dismantling trade protections.

International free-trade agreements (and even regional agreements, such as the North American Free Trade Agreement NAFTA) provide further impetus for trade liberalization. As with SAPs, trade agreements provide governments with political cover for terminating certain protections. (See the related discussion in Chapter 11.1 and 11.2). The GATT in the early post-World War II period led to the reduction of tariffs. The launch of the WTO in 1995 has strengthened the global commitment to free trade (especially among developing countries). The WTO has encouraged governments to consider carefully the costs of any trade intervention, and sets out clear guidelines for the limited and temporary use of protections (see above).

> Trade liberalization may involve short- or medium-term dislocation. But the benefits of liberalization dwarf any induced dislocation.

Trade liberalization may introduce some costs in the short and medium term. Some jobs, firms and even industries may be unable to compete on international markets. The losses incurred are called adjustment costs. But recognition of these costs does not undermine the argument for free trade for three reasons. First, adjustment costs are temporary and small in general, while the gains of trade liberalization are of longer-term nature and much greater than the costs. For example, steel workers who lose their positions once steel is opened to international competition will eventually find employment in the sectors that flourish in the new environment. Second, the aggregate economic gains from trade liberalization outweigh the losses experienced by some groups. Third, governments can compensate the groups that face temporary dislocation due to trade liberalization with the increased resources provided by liberalization.

Rejection of the neoliberal view

> Free trade is not optimal for developing countries, particularly when they are engaged in trade with industrialized countries.

Neoliberals advance their argument for free trade on the basis of the theory of comparative advantage, a theory that they maintain is uncontested by economists in the field of international trade. This is simply not the case. There are important objections to the theory of comparative advantage.

The theory of comparative advantage rests on a host of specific and unrealistic assumptions about technology, industrial structure, macroeconomic conditions, and the mobility of labour and capital. Much research by economists shows that these conditions do not actually obtain in many countries, especially in many developing countries. An important body of international trade theory shows that interventionist trade and industrial policies can be beneficial, and are even compatible within the framework of the theory of comparative advantage (e.g. Krugman 1988).

There are also alternative theories of trade that maintain that the long-term economic performance of developing countries can be harmed by unrestricted trade with industrialized countries. Infant industry theory contends that under free trade poorer countries will specialize in the production of goods that may maximize their income in the short run – this is entirely consistent with the theory of comparative advantage. However, the theory points out that this pattern of specialization stunts long-term growth and development in poorer countries.

Proponents of infant industry theory are therefore quite sceptical of trade between poorer and richer countries. A good illustration of this situation is provided by Mexico's disappointing experience with the NAFTA. The country's experience should serve as a powerful warning for other countries within the Americas that are considering participating in US President Bush's plan to extend the NAFTA southward in the proposed Free Trade Area of the Americas (FTAA). Mexico's experience suggests that developing countries should consider their trade relations with industrialized countries quite carefully. If such trade is to occur, it is imperative that developing countries manage it carefully through the selective use of tariffs and other trade protections and supports (see also Chapter 7.2).

Infant industry theorists argue that developing countries should promote patterns of production (and specialization) that foster long-term economic development. The infant industry argument has a rather long and distinguished lineage. It was first successfully put into practice in Britain following the 1721 trade policy reform of Robert Walpole, the first British Prime Minister. However, it was the first US Treasury Secretary, Alexander Hamilton, in 1791 who first systematically developed the argument.

Following Hamilton, many economists and politicians (among them Abraham Lincoln) in the nineteenth-century USA vigorously contested the British doctrine that free trade is good for all countries and argued that new industries in a less developed country (e.g. the USA at the time) required tariff and other protection in order to develop in the face of stronger competitors from the more advanced countries (e.g. Britain). One US congressman famously remarked in the 1820s that English trade theory, 'like most English manufactured goods, is intended for export, not for consumption at home'.

German economist Friedrich List developed the most sophisticated and forceful elaboration of the infant industry argument in the 1840s after a period of exile in the USA in the 1820s, where he was exposed to Hamilton's argument. List's work inspired the trade and industrial policy in a wide range of countries, from Germany and Japan in the late nineteenth century to numerous developing countries in the post-World War II era.

> Free trade was not how today's industrialized countries developed.

Contrary to the claims of many neoliberals, few countries achieved successful industrial development under free trade (see also Chapter 1). Extensive infant industry protections were central to economic development in Britain in the eighteenth century and the USA in the nineteenth and early twentieth centuries. Nearly all other industrialized countries also used tariffs, export subsidies and other measures of trade protection during the most important moments in their economic development (though not to as great an extent as in Britain or the USA).

During their development, the governments of today's industrialized countries used different combinations of the following policy tools: tariff levies; tariff rebates on imported inputs used in the production of exports; export subsidies; restrictions on the export of the raw materials used by key industries; government regulation of the quality of goods produced for export; and government provision of information on export markets and marketing assistance. Many other countries later used these same policies successfully (e.g. Brazil, India and the East Asian newly industrializing countries [NICs]). The trade policies employed by many of the world's most successful economies run distinctly counter to the free-trade orthodoxy that is so much in vogue today, and that is so heavily promoted (though *not* practised) by industrialized countries.

> The theoretical and statistical support for the neoliberal
> proposition that more open trade leads to faster economic
> growth is extremely weak.

The comparative advantage argument tells us that free trade allows a country to consume more goods than it would if markets were completely closed to international trade. But the increased consumption opportunities that may derive from free trade are not equivalent to the attainment of higher levels of economic growth *over time*. Indeed, there is nothing in the comparative advantage framework that implies that an economy with a more open trade regime, other things equal, will grow faster over time. It is interesting that the most sophisticated of the neoliberal trade economists acknowledge this limitation of the theory of comparative advantage (e.g. Krueger 1980).

The statistical evidence on the growth effects of free trade is also extremely weak (see Evans 1989; Rodriguez and Rodrik 2001). Many of these findings are quite sensitive to the way that trade openness is measured. In some of these studies, trade openness is so generously defined that countries with highly protected trading systems are identified as having a high degree of trade openness. For example, one well-known study by Sachs and Warner (1995) classifies any country with less than a 40 per cent average tariff rate as having an open trade-policy regime. On this questionable basis, the authors conclude that an open trade policy is beneficial to growth. Moreover, only some studies report a positive (though not necessarily strong) statistical *correlation* between greater openness to trade and faster growth. Other studies find no correlation between these factors at all; and still others find an inverse correlation.

A statistical correlation does not prove causation. A statistical correlation between the degree of openness and growth cannot legitimately be interpreted as a finding that more open trade *causes* faster growth. It may be the case that the direction of causality is opposite to that assumed by neoliberals. Under the reverse causality scenario, faster growth and increased productivity may allow countries to open their trade more quickly. This is because the growth in productivity experienced by fast-growing economies may allow them to compete more successfully with more advanced countries, thereby mitigating the need for infant industry protections. Alternatively, a correlation between trade openness and growth (regardless of direction) may not reflect any relationship between these two factors. For example, a developing country may experience negative growth due to a negative external shock (e.g. a rise in oil prices, a reduction in the price of a main export commodity) while pursuing a protectionist trade policy. But this does not imply a causal relationship between growth and trade protection.

Finally, the experiences of individual countries in the post-World War II period cast doubt on the neoliberal view. Among developing countries, the star growth performers of the post-World War II period were countries that did not adopt free trade. Hong Kong and Singapore are obvious exceptions in this regard, but their status as city-states that specialize in international trade makes them special cases. The Singaporean government took an active role in recruiting the types of foreign investment that it identified as important to growth (see Chapter 9.4). Korea, Taiwan and Brazil, countries that grew impressively during the 1960s and 1970s, benefited significantly from strategic trade policies, with the first two countries continuing the impressive growth record under the same policies throughout the 1980s. The star performers of the 1990s, China and India, have also practised strategic trade to great effect. To different degrees, all of these countries mixed targeted tariff protection, subsidies and export promotion, in much the same way that industrialized countries did during their development.

> The dislocation associated with trade liberalization is a far more serious matter than neoliberals acknowledge.

Even if trade liberalization is desirable in a particular context, it nevertheless introduces serious short- and medium-term costs.

Neoliberals acknowledge these costs, but then fail to treat them with the seriousness they deserve.

Trade liberalization necessarily involves the redeployment of resources from sectors that were protected to ones that are not. Neoliberals understate tremendously the cost and time involved in resource reallocation. In the world of economics textbooks, all resources are perfectly mobile and can therefore be reallocated without cost or delay. The reality is that resource reallocation involves economic and human costs and time. Some physical resources, such as a steel mill or an automobile factory, may simply have to be abandoned because they cannot be reshaped into facilities suitable for other uses. Workers may have to be retrained and/or relocated to work in new industries, and this generally cannot be accomplished quickly or cheaply.

Once one takes into account the limited mobility of resources, we can see that trade liberalization can have negative effects on growth, employment and living standards in the short- to medium-run. Spending, output and employment may all contract if certain factories close immediately following trade liberalization. It is also possible that these reductions in economic activity can have ripple effects on other firms and the overall economic environment.

Neoliberals maintain that in time those who are dislocated will find new opportunities, provided that they are flexible and mobile. However, there is no reason to believe that the new opportunities created by trade liberalization will in any sense be better than the opportunities lost, both from an individual and from a social point of view. For example, if the steel workers who lost jobs due to trade liberalization can only find work as janitors, this results not only in a significant fall in their income but also means that the resources that had been invested in forming their skills have stopped generating any return to the society.

Apart from consideration of these short- and medium-term adjustment costs, there is also the problem of compensating those groups/sectors that lose ground in the liberalized trade environment. Most neoliberals believe that such compensation is likely to happen 'naturally', as the newly generated wealth will eventually 'trickle down'. And even those few neoliberals who acknowledge that the trickle-down effect may not be sufficient argue that some minimal and temporary compensation schemes (e.g. minimum social safety net) may be adequate to resolve the problem. But where will the resources for such schemes come from in developing countries, especially when trade liberalization is going to reduce sharply a major source of government revenue – that is, tariff revenue?[3] And how effectively can the groups that are disenfranchised by trade liberalization mobilize politically to demand compensation from the government?[4]

Policy alternatives

> In contrast to neoliberals, we do not offer a single model of trade policy that is universally applicable to all developing countries. However, one basic guideline for trade policy is that it is essential to long-term development that certain industries be protected from international trade competition.

Protective trade barriers – accorded either by tariffs or by other measures such as quotas and subsidies to domestic firms – are critical to industrial development in developing countries. Industrial development and especially the promotion of advanced industries can increase living standards and productivity over the long run in developing countries.

Admittedly, trade protection does have short-run costs (e.g. consumers in developing countries cannot purchase cheaper versions of the same goods produced in industrialized countries). This is especially the case for smaller countries because production on a small scale tends to raise unit costs of production in most industries (though some of these costs can be offset by producing also for export markets). But the short-run costs of trade protection must be weighed against the long-term benefits of creating a vibrant industrial sector.

The outcome of this cost–benefit calculus depends on a number of factors – most importantly, whether domestic producers in the protected industries can be induced to deliver increases in productivity growth, and whether the government can provide complementary supports for industrial development such as education and infrastructure. And like trade liberalization, the adoption of selective trade protection can create dislocation for some workers and industries. The task of providing compensation for these losses, even in the short run, must be taken seriously both for reasons of equity and for the instrumental need to gain broad public support for reform.

The exact form of protection pursued should depend on country size and existing industrial capacities.

Large countries with significant existing industrial capabilities (such as China, India, Brazil and Mexico) may benefit from liberalizing trade in those industries/sectors where domestic producers are internationally competitive. New industries, especially those that are deemed strategic, should be protected until they are internationally competitive. Large developing countries are not terribly dependent on export success because of the size of their domestic market. Nevertheless exports should be promoted (though not at all costs). They not only provide foreign currency earnings, which will enable the purchase of technology from industrialized countries, but they also expose domestic firms to high international quality standards.

Small countries with moderate industrial bases would benefit from more explicit efforts to link infant industry protection with export promotion. The domestic markets of smaller countries are inadequate to support a diverse range of industries. It is therefore important that smaller countries engage in selective export promotion. Export-promotion programmes may vary in content. Some types of export promotion are permissible under current WTO rules. For example, export subsidies are only allowed under the

WTO for the poorest countries, by which is meant countries with per capita income below $1,000 (approximately). However, tariff rebates on the inputs used for export production are still possible under the WTO. Thus, this scheme can be more actively utilized as a means of promoting exports (much as it was by eighteenth-century Britain and post-World War II Korea and Taiwan).[5]

Business subsidies that are unrelated to exports are still allowed by the WTO. Policymakers can find creative ways to ensure that broader business subsidies benefit export performance indirectly. For example, governments can establish an industrial park in a depressed region and provide the businesses that locate there with subsidies for regional development. Some of these firms might produce goods for the domestic market with an eye towards future export success. The government trading agencies can provide information and marketing support for exporters, especially the smaller firms. The government can also court export-oriented TNCs by establishing export-processing zones (EPZs) or can provide TNCs with subsidies that are unrelated to exports (however, see the caveats in Chapter 9.4).

Very poor countries with little to no industrial base face the most significant challenges, but also have the greatest latitude within WTO rules. Very poor countries may benefit from protection of and subsidies to more basic types of manufacturing industries (such as textiles, food-processing), as even these may not be internationally competitive absent government protection. Resources for the support of basic manufacturing industries can be drawn from the revenues of primary product exports. Very poor countries can use export subsidies under WTO rules. Every effort should therefore be made to exploit this advantage in the drive to produce the maximum possible volume of basic manufactures for export. Enlarging the scale of production in the export sector has two main benefits: the country earns the maximum possible volume of foreign currency via exports; and the unit costs of production in the export sector can be reduced. Governments that employ this strategy, however, must also design a transition strategy that can move the country into more sophisticated manufactures over time.

> Current WTO rules do not preclude all interventionist trade policies. Moreover, the rules are subject to interpretation and negotiation.

The free-trade vision of the WTO does not serve the aspirations of many developing countries. The governance mechanisms of the WTO bias its decisions in favour of the industrialized countries with regard to both agenda-setting and agreement implementation. The WTO has also made it harder for developing countries to use trade protections.

Nevertheless there is room for some types of trade protection under present WTO rules. While many countries have reduced their tariffs dramatically and have established ceilings on maximum tariff rates under their WTO obligations, these ceilings remain at non-trivial rates of 20–30 per cent. Tariffs of this magnitude have the capacity to influence trade and production patterns in many industries.

There are some types of subsidies that are still permissible by the WTO – these subsidies are 'non-actionable' in the language of the WTO. Subsidies for basic research and development (R&D) and subsidies to help economically disadvantaged regions are non-actionable under the WTO. Indeed, many industrialized countries subsidize their industries under the guise of R&D support or regional policies.

Developing countries can also impose temporary controls on trade either at the sectoral level (say, due to a rapid influx of imports in particular industries) or at the economy-wide level in the event of balance-of-payments difficulties. In the case of a balance-of-payments problem, the government has substantial latitude in determining exactly what type of controls to impose on which sectors, thus enabling them to use these controls for broader industrial policy purposes. Of course, it should be noted that the WTO mandates that the severity of the controls must be commensurate with the scale of the balance-of-payments problem.

Finally, as in any legal framework, WTO rules are statements of broad principles. As such, WTO rules must be actively interpreted through dispute settlement panels. This introduces the possibility of collective action by developing countries (especially with some of the largest of these taking leadership). They might press for interpretations of WTO rules in ways that are more beneficial to their interests. Also, the appointment of former Thai economic minister Mr Supachai as the new director-general of the WTO means that the process of 'legally interpreting' WTO agreements may have, on the margin, become more favourable to developing countries.

WTO rules are not immutable.

The WTO agreement can and should be rewritten to make it more amenable to interventionist trade policies by developing countries (see Conclusion). Here, too, collective action by developing countries would be helpful in pressing this agenda. There are also some industrialized countries, such as France and Japan, where free-trade ideology has far less sway than it does in the USA and Britain. These countries might be useful allies in an effort to rework the WTO agreement in important areas.

7.2 **Industrial Policy**

Terminology

Industrial policy is more precisely termed selective industrial policy. Selective industrial policy refers to policies that favour the development of certain industries or sectors over others with a view to enhancing national economic welfare in the long run (Chang, 1994: ch.3). This may be accomplished through a range of policies, such as trade subsidies; licenses; and the management of credit and capital allocation, prices and investment.

The neoliberal view

States should not shape industrial development.

As in the case of trade policy (see Chapter 7.1), governments should not allocate resources because these decisions will be distorted by political considerations and will induce efficiencies. This is a problem in all countries, but it is especially serious in developing countries where state officials are more likely to be corrupt and/or incompetent (see also Chapter 11).

The market mechanism is capable of optimally allocating economic resources, outside a few exceptional areas. There are instances when markets do not allocate resources optimally – they are called 'market failures'. In the case of market failure, state intervention may improve social welfare. But such market failures are rare and mainly occur in areas like infrastructure (e.g. roads), legal protections (e.g. contract enforcement) and scientific research, rather than in industries.[6]

Selective industrial policy creates inefficiency, introduces channels for corruption, hampers innovation, and compromises long-term growth and social welfare.

Market failures rarely exist within the industrial sector. If the state intervenes where market failures do not exist (with price caps or subsidies), it will distort resource allocation by interfering with price signals. For example, subsidies to a particular industry artificially inflate profits in that industry. Consequently, entrepreneurs shift out of other industries into the subsidized industry. The total output of the subsidized industry will rise, even though there is no increase in the level of consumer demand for the products of that industry. (This argument is analogous to that advanced against trade protection; see Chapter 7.1.)

Selective industrial policy also hampers innovation – that is, the generation of new products, production processes or managerial techniques. Entrepreneurs will be discouraged from innovating if the government proscribes their behaviour and/or eliminates the rewards for taking risks. Indeed, the long-term economic costs of diminished innovation may overshadow even the short-term inefficiencies associated with selective industrial policy.

Finally, selective industrial policy creates political problems. Selective industrial policy requires a bureaucracy to administer it. An empowered bureaucracy can be a drag on growth for a number of reasons. Bureaucrats can make it difficult to conduct business in an efficient manner because they create costly and time-consuming regulations, partly to justify their jobs but also to create more power to extract bribes. In such an environment, the private sector must devote considerable resources to lobbying, which diverts talents from more 'productive' activities like R&D.

> The experience of developing countries demonstrates that selective industrial policies do not work and are economically harmful.

During the 1950s–1970s, many developing countries implemented selective industrial policies as part of their failed ISI programmes. Rapid industrialization was seen as a key to state-building and modernization. In many cases, the legacy of colonialism also fuelled the desire to develop a strong, independent industrial sector.

The economic theories of the ascendant Structuralist school in Latin America and the 'Big Push model' associated with economists Paul Rosenstein-Rodan, Ragnar Nurkse and Tibor Scitovsky provided the intellectual foundation for ISI programmes and the selective industrial policies that were associated with them. The Structuralist school was led by Raul Prebisch, the former governor of Argentina's central bank and the director of the UN's Economic Commission for Latin America (ECLA).

Structuralism argued that developing countries could not develop an industrial base without trade protection and selective industrial policy. At the same time, the Big Push model argued that industrialization in developing countries could succeed only if the state promoted related industries simultaneously. Without this coordinated effort, domestic industries would have neither sufficient demand for their products nor sufficient supplies of the inputs that are necessary for the production process.

Many governments in the developing world adopted the complementary ideas of Structuralism and Big Push models between the 1950s and the 1970s (and in some cases into the 1980s). This resulted in the widespread adoption of selective industrial policies. For example, in India, Prime Minister Nehru's regime pursued an aggressive programme that sought to accelerate industrial development in the long run by forcing resources into industries that produced capital goods.

Such policies were unmitigated failures. These programmes failed to achieve their most basic objective of promoting sustained industrialization and ending the dependence on industrialized countries. These programmes also required so much foreign borrowing that they led to the debt crisis of the 1980s.

Industrial policy – if used – must be general.

As in the case of trade protection, developing countries should employ only general – rather than selective – industrial policy (see Chapter 7.1). General industrial policy means that governments should intervene in ways that do not favour any single industry. Examples include the provision of basic education and infrastructure and support for broad R&D.

While competition policy is a legitimate component of general industrial policy, it should be very carefully deployed. Competition policy involves anti-trust legislation (that prevents abuses by monopolistic firms) and the creation of regulatory bodies. Given that these regulatory bodies are apt to be corrupted by lobbying ('regulatory capture'), it is vital to create politically independent regulatory agencies that operate with little discretion, if competition policy is to succeed (see also Chapter 11).

Rejection of the neoliberal view

> There are many economic theories that provide a rationale for selective industrial policy.

The rejection of selective industrial policy by neoliberals follows directly from their theory of international trade and their understanding of states and markets (see Chapters 7.1, 1 and 6). Once we move beyond these incomplete and biased understandings we find that there are many sound theoretical reasons for selective industrial policy.

There is a large body of economic theory and empirical research that demonstrates that market actors tend to underestimate the long-term gains of particular activities, such as R&D (see Chapters 9 and 10). Thus it is often necessary to offer government support for activities that both take a long time to bear fruit and are of national importance.

Research has also shown that markets are not always able to value externalities appropriately. (See note 6 for a definition and discussion of externalities.) For example, industry-specific R&D may positively influence technological development in a broad range of industries. In such circumstances, government support for specific, and not just 'basic', R&D is appropriate.

In keeping with the Big Push theory, markets are not always adequate to the task of coordinating large, interdependent decisions. Governments can therefore play an important role in co-ordinating *complementary* investment decisions. At the same time, it is also true that markets often fail to coordinate *competing* investment decisions. This kind of coordination failure can lead to duplicative investments or overcapacity, and hence falling prices for the oversupplied good (Chang 2001). The consequences of duplicative investments cannot always be overcome quickly or easily as, for example, steel mills cannot readily be transformed into textile mills. The state can play an important role in preventing excessive duplication of investment.

The track record of selective industrial policies in both
industrialized and developing countries is far more impressive
than neoliberals are wont to acknowledge.

The successful use of selective industrial policy in the East Asian
countries such as Japan, South Korea and Taiwan is well known
(on Japan, see Johnson 1982; on Korea, see Amsden 1989; on
Taiwan, see Wade 1990). In these countries, governments used a
judicious mix of state intervention and market incentives (especially
in relation to export markets) to promote a range of domestic
industries. Governments also used a host of policy measures to
modernize the industrial structure and increase productivity. These
included: infant industry protections; export and other business
subsidies; directed credit (in which state-controlled banks provided
subsidized credit to designated industries); indicative investment
planning;[7] regulation and coordination of industrial investment;
and both targeted and general support for R&D and training. The
world-class automobile, steel and electronics industries in Japan
and Korea, and electronics and chemicals in Taiwan, would not
have developed without industrial policy.

Moreover, the success of selective industrial policy is not
confined to East Asia. Other developing countries also used the
policy with success. The Brazilian aerospace industry is the most
notable example. During the post-World War II period, a number
of European countries, notably France, Austria, Norway and
Finland, aggressively used selective industrial policy (Chang 1994:
ch. 3). These countries used indicative investment planning, state
control over finance, state-owned enterprises, various trade control
measures, and industrial subsidies to modernize their industries and
compete with and eventually surpass countries like the UK.

Finally, it bears mentioning that industrial policies in East
Asia and Europe were never *anti-market*. Their industrial policies
involved the selective control of market forces. The control of
market forces was designed to enhance the ability of national
firms to compete in the world market.

Implementation problems are largely responsible for the failure of selective industrial policies in some countries.

Selective industrial policies have not succeeded everywhere. Nearly all of the instances of policy failure are marked by the absence of appropriate mechanisms of accountability, performance review and oversight. Failure has occurred when the government has granted trade protection and/or subsidies to certain industries without monitoring performance and without tying support to performance guidelines. In these contexts, selective industrial policy usually did not lead to enhanced performance.

Successful experiences with selective industrial policy are very much tied to the government's commitment to monitoring and performance targets (Amsden 1989; Johnson 1982). For example, in Korea and Japan firms had to prove that they were using state support to increase productivity and/or exports. If they failed to do so, they were penalized through the withdrawal of state support in subsequent periods.

The importance of competent, committed civil servants to the success of selective industrial policy programmes is a concern for developing countries. Surely a government's ability to monitor and discipline the recipients of support depends on the ability of civil servants to carry out the government's vision. Some analysts have suggested that this level of state autonomy and capacity can exist only when dictators are in power. The experiences of South Korea and Taiwan are frequently invoked in this regard. But the positive experience of many democratic countries with selective industrial policy suggests that dictatorships are not a prerequisite for public employee competence and policy success. Japan, France, Austria, Norway and Finland are democratic countries that have used selective industrial policy effectively.

Other analysts have suggested that competent, honest government officials are a product of a country's unique history. But this is not always the case. Some countries created a competent cadre of civil servants through political, economic and administrative reforms. For example, prior to World War II French civil servants were highly conservative and strongly averse to intervention. But after World War II the views of the government on intervention changed dramatically. The act of implementing interventionist policies transformed the French civil service – indeed, it quickly became among the most dynamic and forward-looking in the world (Cohen 1977). Until the 1950s, Korean civil servants were considered to be highly corrupt and incompetent (Chang 1994: ch. 4). This, too, changed rather quickly as the economic policy regime changed (see Chapter 5).[8]

> The neoliberal argument that only general industrial policies should be pursued is rather difficult to understand since very few industrial policy measures are truly general.

Beyond support for primary and lower-secondary education it is difficult to imagine what kinds of policy interventions would not benefit one type of industry over another. For example, support for R&D will be of greater benefit to high-technology industries than to the textile industry. Alternatively, government support for programmes to train skilled workers must be oriented towards some industries over others. It is difficult to imagine a general engineering training programme that is not targeted towards producing some specific type of engineer (e.g. chemical over electrical engineers).

Policy alternatives

> As with trade policy, there is no single template for selective industrial policy across developing countries.

There are many paths to industrialization. There is the option of building a broad industrial base on the basis of strong infant industry protection with the help of an aggressive export strategy. This was the path to industrialization taken by Japan and South Korea. In countries that are well endowed with natural resources it may be appropriate to build an industrial base that has close links to the resource base. This was the path taken by the Scandinavian countries. In other countries, industrialization may be accomplished by strategically attracting TNCs in technologically dynamic industries (see Chapters 8.2 and 9.4). The industrialization strategy of Singapore and Ireland relied on this approach.

> The first step in the design of a selective industrial policy is the design of an overall 'development vision' for the country.

It is critical that policymakers carefully identify their country's endowments of natural and human resources and competencies (e.g. the strengths of the country's producers), and examine conditions in international and regional markets. These factors should figure prominently in the design of a development vision for their country.

The design of a development vision may be facilitated by thinking in terms of the models of industrialization used by early success stories. For instance, policymakers could think in terms of an 'American', 'Scandinavian', 'German', 'Japanese/Korean' or 'Singaporean' model of industrialization. Needless to say, these models should be considered heuristic devices only. We are not implying that an imported model should be blindly followed.

At early stages of development all developing countries have (relative) strengths in natural-resource-related activities. For example, the largest export item of notoriously response-poor Korea in the 1950s was tungsten ore. However, manufacturing capabilities can be built even in areas with no obvious 'natural' linkages – after all, Korea does not produce iron ore or coking coal, two key inputs into steel-making. But the country has nevertheless developed one of the world's most efficient steel industries.

> Once an industrial strategy has been developed, the second step is to design policies in other areas that will facilitate the industrial policy.

It is essential that macroeconomic and financial policies encourage investment (see Chapters 10, 11). This is key to industrial upgrading and long-term competitiveness. Education, infrastructure, public investment and technology policy must also support industrial policy (on public investment, see Chapter 11.3). If, for example, policymakers want to develop an electronics industry, resources will have to be channelled to departments of electronic engineering at universities, while there should also be investments in electricity and telecommunications networks.

> The third step involves design of clear performance targets and incentives to fulfil these targets. This requires building requisite implementation capabilities – both human and institutional.

It is important to design industrial policy in such a way that the possibility of implementation failure is minimized. Clear performance targets are essential in this regard.

The design of appropriate performance targets will depend on the particular industry involved. In countries like Japan, Korea and Taiwan, targets typically focused on export growth, increases in local content and R&D capabilities, and increases in the ability to withstand import competition. It is widely agreed that export-based performance targets have the advantage of providing easily verifiable and relatively objective performance criteria, although they should not be the only criterion. Also, performance targets must be set realistically. This necessitates dialogue between firms, industries and government. Care must be taken, however, to avoid establishing targets that are too low, which is likely to happen if the private sector has its own way.

The design and monitoring of performance targets require a competent civil service, something that is not readily available in many developing countries. The quality of the civil service in developing countries can be enhanced through organizational reform and through enhanced employee skills. In this connection it is important to note that this does not necessarily imply that better-educated economists must be hired. The civil servants who deftly managed industrial policy in East Asia were mostly lawyers (in Japan and, to a lesser extent, in Korea) and engineers (in Taiwan and China).

Rewards and penalties must be tied to performance targets. This can introduce political problems and lobbying, especially where penalties for failing to meet targets are involved. But the experience of a number of countries (some with democratic and some with dictatorial regimes) shows that these political pressures can be overcome. What is required is a programme to forge consensus on a long-term developmental strategy that includes industrial policy as one of its components.

Notes

1. In the academic literature, the terms 'openness' or 'outward orientation' are more frequently used than the terms 'free trade' or 'less restricted trade'. We use these terms interchangeably.
2. In their influential 1970 book, long regarded as the seminal neoliberal work on trade policy in developing countries, Little, Scott and Scitovsky argue that the justifiable tariff rate is near zero for the more advanced developing countries, and is at most 20 per cent for even the poorest developing countries (1970: 159).
3. Because tariffs are easy to collect, developing country governments with weak tax administration tend to rely more heavily on tariff revenue than the governments of more developed countries with better tax administration (see Chapter 11.3).
4. Disenfranchised corn growers in Mexico have been unable to press the government to compensate them for the significant losses they have experienced thanks to opening the Mexican market to corn exports from the USA under the provisions of the NAFTA. As a result, the NAFTA has meant a serious decline in the standard of living of small farmers in Mexico.
5. However, this tool is effective only where there is a substantial tariff on the input concerned.
6. Two classes of market failure are most frequently mentioned. They are public goods and externalities. Public goods are so named because once they are provided they have to be made available to the entire public, and not just to those individuals who have paid for them. This is because you cannot exclude people from enjoying the benefits of public goods. For example, you cannot devise a national defence system that allows an invading army to occupy only the houses of individuals who have failed to pay for national defence.

Knowing this, individuals would not purchase a national defence system if it were offered through a market, even if they wanted a defence system. For this reason, governments provide the public good of national defence. Externalities are the effects of a particular activity on parties that are not involved in it. Scientific research, for example, benefits those who have not paid for it by expanding the available pool of knowledge. It is therefore in society's interest for the government to stimulate more scientific research than might be generated by market incentives alone.

7. Indicative investment planning refers to the practice wherein the government 'indicates' where it wants to encourage investment through a well-publicized plan. The plan is not 'mandatory' in the sense of Soviet-style planning. But the plan has the effect of channelling investment into areas of government priority, because the government encourages this through subsidies and other supports and because this exercise provides 'focal points' around which private investors coordinate complementary activities.

8. Of course, the quality of the civil service is not the only factor that determines the success of a country's industrial policy. Another key factor is the coherence of the government's overall development plan, of which selective industrial policy is just one component. For example, without substantial capital controls and a certain degree of financial regulation, selective industrial policy is unlikely to succeed (see Chapters 9, 10).

8 **Policy Alternatives 2**

Privatization and
Intellectual Property Rights

8.1 **Privatization**

Terminology

Neoliberals promote a policy of privatization, a policy that involves moving resources and enterprises from public to private ownership. This transfer in ownership is accomplished through the sale of assets formerly held by the state. In some cases, sales take place through capital markets, such that private investors purchase shares of former state-owned enterprises (SOEs). In other cases, SOEs are simply sold intact to private bidders. In some former socialist countries, privatization was accomplished through 'vouchers'. All citizens were given a certain number of shares in all major SOEs; these shares could then be freely traded on capital markets. Voucher privatization enabled new post-socialist governments to privatize rapidly.

The neoliberal view

> SOEs suffer from chronic inefficiencies, waste and
> mismanagement.

SOEs suffer from chronic problems of inefficiency, waste and mismanagement because of peculiarities in their ownership, management, incentive and market structures. The managers of SOEs do not own the enterprises they run. As mere 'hired hands', SOE managers have no incentive to run efficient enterprises and even less of an incentive to improve their efficiency.

Privately owned firms are not immune from the 'hired hands problem' since managers of these firms rarely own them. But the problem is far less serious in the private sector because management performance is monitored by shareholders and checked by market incentives and competition. Stock options, which give managers an ownership stake in the firms they run, also strengthen the incentive for them to perform well. In addition, the liquidity of capital markets gives shareholders the ability to penalize firms for poor performance by selling their stockholdings. The threat that shareholders will sell shares of underperforming firms serves to discipline firm managers.

There is also the potential for underperforming firms in the private sector to be bought by other firms (by virtue of what is termed the takeover mechanism). This may occur because the stock prices of underperforming firms fall when shareholders sell their holdings. In this instance, the underperforming management team may lose their posts once the firm is purchased. The threat of job loss is another source of management discipline. Finally, firms in the private sector must compete for market share. This, too, encourages management to do their jobs effectively.

By contrast, managers in SOEs face none of these pressures. There are no real shareholders in SOEs as they rarely even have shares (because, in technical terms, they are not incorporated). Even in those few cases where SOEs do have shares, they are usually not traded on the stock market. Thus, the threat of shareholder exit cannot be brought to bear on SOE management. Of course, technically, the general public is a kind of shareholder in SOEs because they elect the government that appoints SOE management. But such indirect channels exert little pressure on management.

Many SOEs are monopolies within a particular sector, sometimes by law. This status exacerbates the tendency of SOEs to produce shoddy products and maintain high prices and low standards of service.[1]

Large SOE sectors have taken a toll on developing economies.

Operating SOEs is a costly endeavour, one that wastes scarce budgetary resources. These costs contribute to budget imbalance and inflation in developing countries (see Chapter 11.3). Indeed, the government borrowing that was necessary to sustain SOEs in many countries contributed to the debt crisis of the 1980s.

The case against SOEs is also supported by numerous case studies. For example, a key report on SOEs by the World Bank opens with several striking facts. The report states that in Tanzania, central government subsidies to SOEs respectively account for 72 and 150 per cent of central government spending on education and health. In Indonesia, government factories discharge about five times as much water pollution per unit of output as do private factories of the same size and age that are engaged in the same activity. In Egypt, Peru, Senegal and Turkey, a mere 5 per cent reduction in SOE operating costs would reduce the fiscal deficit by about one-third (World Bank 1995: 1–2).

Many statistical studies show that the relative size of a country's SOE sector is negatively correlated with economic growth. These studies imply that the larger the SOE sector, the more inefficient is the economy. Consequently, economies with large SOE sectors grow more slowly.

Recently, most developing countries have come to embrace the virtues of private enterprise and have privatized many SOEs.

In the early days of the post-colonial period, leaders of newly sovereign nations believed that SOEs would play a leading role in economic independence and modernization. In this context, many countries confiscated and nationalized enterprises owned by former colonial powers and also established numerous SOEs.

Since the 1980s, policymakers in many developing countries have recognized the failings of SOEs, and accordingly have privatized aggressively. By the late 1980s, new post-socialist leaders embraced privatization.

Rejection of the neoliberal view

There are many reasons to question the neoliberal view that SOE managers necessarily perform poorly relative to their private-sector counterparts.

Neoliberal claims about the superiority of the incentive, reward and monitoring practices in the private sector are unsupportable.

Research shows that managers in private firms are often driven to maximize their firm's current stock price (at any cost), especially if they are compensated with stock options. But this management objective may not serve the long-term interests of the firm or of the broader economy (see also Chapters 4, 9.3 and 10).

In their embrace of the takeover mechanism, neoliberals ignore the fact that takeovers are rare outside of the USA and the UK. In a great many countries, takeovers are either banned by law or are rare because of social custom. Moreover, takeovers do not necessarily encourage sound management in the private sector. Many studies find that the threat of takeovers is another reason why managers in the USA and UK focus excessively on current stock prices. These same studies find that when takeovers do occur, the new firm that is created rarely performs better than the old firm in regard to profitability and efficiency.

Additionally, it is rarely possible for numerous, dispersed shareholders to monitor management performance in the private firms in which they hold relatively small stakes. There is a kind of public good problem here: although all shareholders can collectively benefit from improved managerial performance, no individual shareholder has sufficient incentive to monitor and discipline management on her/his own (see Chapter 7 note 6 on public goods).

In fact, it may be easier to monitor SOEs as compared to firms in the private sector. On the one hand, the public – being made up of taxpayers whose contributions will be squandered if SOEs are inefficiently managed – has at least as great an incentive to discipline errant SOE managers as do shareholders in the private sector. On the other hand, the centralized structure in which SOEs operate makes monitoring them easier. In the SOE sector a few agencies (such as a public enterprise agency or a public holding company) are responsible for SOE performance. It may therefore be easier for a centralized agency to monitor management performance than for numerous, dispersed shareholders to do so.

Some SOEs do face competition in product markets.

Neoliberals often claim that SOEs are inefficient because they operate as monopolies, and therefore do not face competition in product markets. But not all SOEs occupy this position. In many countries, SOEs compete vigorously with private-sector firms.[2] For example, in France the auto manufacturer Renault, which was nationalized following the end of World War II and remained an SOE until 1996, faced direct competition from the private firm Peugeot as well as from foreign producers.[3]

To be sure, some SOEs are statutory monopolies. But even SOEs of this sort face competition from private-sector firms that provide partly substitutable products and services. For example, during the 1980s the state-owned railway company of Britain faced rather intense competition from privately owned bus companies in some segments of their market. During the late 1980s and the early 1990s, South Korea had two state-owned telephone companies that engaged in vigorous competition with one another.

Empirical evidence does not support the claim that SOEs undermine growth.

Neoliberals frequently draw reference to anecdotal and statistical studies that show that the presence of SOEs hampers economic growth. But empirical evidence does not bear this out.

A number of economies with large SOE sectors have performed very well during the post-World War II period. In France, Austria, Finland, Norway and Italy, a dynamic SOE sector played a key role in industrial development. The SOE sector in these countries has been among the largest in the industrialized world. And while correlation most definitely does not prove causation, it is nevertheless interesting to note that these economies all grew impressively for many decades after World War II. Between the 1950s and the 1980s, Austria enjoyed a 3.9 per cent annual rate of growth in per capita income, which placed it second among the sixteen large advanced economies. Italy came in at fourth place with annual growth of 3.7 per cent; Finland was fifth (3.6 per cent), Norway was sixth (3.4 per cent), and France was seventh (3.2 per cent).[4]

Some of the most successful economies in East Asia also had large SOE sectors. The most important example in this regard is Taiwan, a country that has had one of the largest SOE sectors in the developing world (outside of the oil-producing countries).[5] Taiwan has been the fastest growing economy in the world during the post-World War II period. This impressive performance was surely not solely caused by SOEs, but it does seem that a large SOE sector did not cause the country to perform poorly (as neoliberals would have it). Singapore and South Korea also had large SOE sectors (indeed, Korea's was comparable in relative size to that of India). These countries were star growth performers despite the presence of large SOE sectors. Notably, the Korean SOE that produces steel, POSCO, became the most efficient producer in the world barely ten years after the firm was established in the early 1970s.[6]

In Africa, the SOE sector plays almost as large a role in market-oriented and successful economies such as Ivory Coast and Kenya as in socialist Tanzania. Overall, the successful economies in Asia have larger SOE sectors than do the economies in Latin America that are relatively weak performers.

In sum: it has proven nearly impossible to establish an unambiguous causal empirical link between the size of the SOE sector and economic growth. We can safely say, however, that there is no evidence that a large SOE sector necessarily causes countries to perform poorly.

Case studies that try to compare the performance of SOEs and private enterprises operating under similar conditions (e.g. similar industries, similar firm sizes) are also inconclusive. These studies tend to concentrate on countries with poorly performing SOEs. This method of case selection does not provide us with a full picture of SOE performance.

An SOE sector has a place in all economies.

There are some resources that should *always* be in the public domain and should remain under national control. Products and services that are essential to human life (such as water, utilities, sanitation, basic education and communications) and critical natural resources should always be under the control of the government. The privatization of water systems in the developing world is an unmitigated disaster for the vast majority of the population in these countries.

SOEs are often the best way to deal with what are called natural monopolies. Natural monopolies occur where the required scale of investment is so large that it only makes economic sense for one firm to operate in a particular market. Utilities (such as electricity distribution) are an example of a natural monopoly.

Even in industries without a natural monopoly, SOEs are often the only organizations capable of undertaking large-scale projects because of their cost and managerial prerequisites. This is particularly the case in many developing countries where financial resources are scarce and where entrepreneurs in the private sector can sometimes be extremely risk-averse. This was the situation in France, Austria and Taiwan prior to the creation of large SOE sectors. Prior to World War II, private businesspeople in these countries were particularly risk-averse. But following the nationalization of many key industries after World War II, governments in these countries installed dynamic and forward-looking managers in SOEs. These SOEs played a central role in industrial modernization.

SOEs are often better able to take externalities into account, as they can look beyond financial profitability (see Chapter 7 note 6 on externalities). In some cases, it may be easier for the government to ensure that SOEs address social objectives (such as regional income disparities) because of their influence over SOE management.

> Privatization is certainly appropriate in some contexts, but the implementation process can be costly and difficult to manage.

There are several factors that policymakers should consider when designing privatization programmes (where such programmes are appropriate). It is often the case that governments seek to sell the least profitable SOE, while the private sector seeks to purchase the most profitable. In order to create interest in a poorly performing SOE, the government often has to invest heavily in it. If these efforts are successful, there is the question of why the SOE should then be sold.

It is often the case that it costs quite a bit of money and time to sell an SOE on the stock market. The valuation of an SOE and the flotation of its shares on the stock market can be a significant burden on the resources of the government. This matter is particularly complicated when the country does not have a well-functioning stock market (in which case shares have to be listed on overseas markets). Moreover, foreign ownership of certain domestic resources can be a problem in its own right.

Many governments inaugurate privatization as a means of raising revenue. But studies show that privatization is not the boon to government budgets that is often thought (see Chapter 11.3). SOEs are frequently sold for bargain prices to foreign investors or domestic 'insiders'. These deals have sometimes been accompanied by a fair bit of corruption.

Policy alternatives

> Governments should consider carefully the economic rationale for privatization.

Many SOEs in developing countries are performing well. These should not be privatized. Many governments have engaged in privatization to signal their commitment to broader market reform or to address short- or medium-term budgetary shortfalls. The former goal can be accomplished through other means, and in any case is of questionable legitimacy. Some countries have proven quite adept at attracting foreign investment despite the presence of large SOE sectors. The latter goal of addressing budgetary gaps can be accomplished more effectively through fiscal reform (see Chapter 11.3).

> Governments should also consider the costs of privatization.

As argued above, it can be expensive to initiate privatization programmes. There is also the matter of distributional, political and social costs, especially as concerns vulnerable groups within society. At the very least, these costs suggest that the government is obligated to make significant transfers to economically vulnerable groups that are harmed by privatization. A full assessment of the costs of privatization may lead many governments to pursue this reform with far less vigour.

> There are many ways to improve the performance of SOEs without privatization.

The first involves what can be called organizational reform. Very often SOEs are charged with serving too many objectives (e.g. social goals, industrialization and the provision of basic services), and the relative importance of each goal is unclear. These ambiguities can cause management to lose focus, and efficiency suffers accordingly. The solution is obvious: governments should clarify the mandate of particular SOEs and hold management accountable to well-defined mandates.

Another important element of organizational reform involves improving the quality of information and monitoring of SOE performance. In many countries, the agencies that supervise SOEs lack the information and skills to monitor SOE performance (e.g. in some countries SOEs don't even produce balance sheets). Improving the flow of information and supervisory competence is a critical objective of SOE reform.

There is also the need for some reform of the incentive and monitoring system within which SOEs operate. A system of clear incentives should be designed that rewards managers and employees for improvements in efficiency, productivity and consumer satisfaction. The establishment of a single and competently staffed agency that is dedicated to SOE supervision could also improve monitoring. On paper, many SOEs today are monitored by multiple agencies. In practice, this can mean that they are supervised by no agency. Consolidation of monitoring responsibility could increase its efficiency and could also make it clear where blame lies when monitoring turns out to be inadequate. The same point could pertain to SOEs themselves. There are cases where performance could be improved through the consolidation of duplicative SOEs.

Some types of competition may prove beneficial to SOE performance. In particular, some SOEs have performed well when related (though not duplicative) competitors have been privatized. As in the case of the Korean telecommunications industry (see above), competition between SOEs can also be beneficial.

In some contexts, political reform may be the best way to improve SOE performance. In some countries, SOEs are used to create employment and income in particular regions or for certain groups. For example, SOEs are used to promote employment in poor regions of Southern Italy, and were used to create employment for white South Africans during apartheid. SOEs are not the best means to address problems that require a political solution. In the case of Southern Italy, for example, mechanisms that transfer wealth from the North to the South of the country could be a more effective and appropriate means for addressing underdevelopment in the South.

8.2 **Intellectual Property Rights**

Terminology

Intellectual property rights (IPRs) are rights over ideas. They are codified in patents, copyrights and trademarks.

The neoliberal view

> IPRs are essential to investment and growth.

IPRs are just like other types of property rights. Absent the protection of IPRs, there will be no incentive for investors to risk their resources in the generation of new ideas or new products. For example, a pharmaceuticals company will only have an incentive to invest in the development of new medicines if it enjoys the sole right to the profits on sales of the new medicine. Likewise, consumers will be unwilling to pay a premium price for Nike products if the company's trademark were not protected. Without trademark protection, consumers could not be certain if they were purchasing counterfeit goods.

Patents and other IPRs were critical to innovation and investment in industrialized countries during their development. Patent laws were implemented in the eighteenth-century USA, Britain and France precisely because governments recognized the importance of this protection to the generation of new knowledge, inventions and technological progress. For these same reasons, virtually all other European and North American countries adopted patent laws by the mid-nineteenth century. As the US National Law Center for Inter-American Free Trade put it: '[t]he historical record in the industrialized countries, which began as developing countries, demonstrates that [IPR] protection has been one of the most powerful instruments for economic development, export growth, and the diffusion of new technologies, art and culture' (1997: 1).

> The WTO has strengthened the protection of IPRs. Contrary to a popular view, this will benefit the developing countries.

Until quite recently, developing countries routinely ignored patents and other IPRs, despite national laws governing these matters. For example, Indian drug companies produced cheap copies of Western drugs that were immensely expensive to develop initially. Korean firms produced counterfeit luxury goods, such as Gucci bags, and thereby helped to devalue the status of their brands.

Today, developing countries must protect IPRs to the degree that they are protected in industrialized countries. Thanks to the trade-related intellectual property rights (TRIPS) agreement of the WTO, many countries must extend patents to formerly unprotected areas, such as pharmaceutical products (as opposed to pharmaceutical processes, which were already protected in many developing countries). Under the TRIPS agreement, many developing countries are required to extend patent life to twenty years. The TRIPS agreement allows countries that have been harmed by IPR violations to impose trade sanctions on violating countries.

The opposition of many governments in the developing world to the TRIPS agreement is short-sighted. True, developing countries now have to pay substantial royalties to obtain patent licences, but the numerous medium- to long-run benefits that accrue from IPR protection far outweigh the economic costs of TRIPS payments. First, protection of IPRs encourages innovation and foreign investment. Second, enforcement of TRIPS makes it easier for developing countries to gain access to advanced technologies and products. This is because inventors and investors will no longer fear that they will be denied their rightful profits because of IPR violations. Third, firms in industrialized countries will be more willing to create products and technologies specifically for developing countries (such as medicines to fight tropical diseases) now that they no longer fear IPR violations.

Rejection of the neoliberal view

> The protection of private IPRs is not a prerequisite for the generation of new knowledge in all circumstances.

Before turning to other matters, we consider first the exact meaning and implication of IPRs in the neoliberal view. For neoliberals, only *private* actors are to enjoy IPRs. In other words, neoliberals argue that individuals or corporations as legal persons should be granted property rights over ideas. They argue that there will be no incentive for innovation, investment and technological progress absent the possibility that monetary profits will accrue to individuals or firms. Left out of the neoliberal notion of IPRs is the possibility that 'social profit' or social welfare can serve as an incentive for innovation, or that government should possess IPRs.

There are many cases where ideas have been generated without monetary gain in mind. In such circumstances, we might consider the idea of *public* or *communal* property rights. One example of this type of public property right occurs in the open software programs (sometimes called freeware) that are available on the Internet. The principles behind open software are straightforward: it is shared freely with the public at no charge; users can improve upon it; and users are expected to share the improved software with the public. The only proviso is that no one can exploit the software for commercial gain. From a neoliberal perspective, open software is illogical in so far as it involves a significant investment of ideas for reasons other than monetary gain.

In this connection, it is interesting to note that many prominent nineteenth-century thinkers made a case for the public ownership of ideas. Thomas Jefferson, the first Secretary of State of the USA and the country's third President, argued that ideas were 'like air' and should not be owned by individuals.[7] Many of the same nineteenth-century economists that advocated free trade also advocated the elimination of patents because they were thought to create a type of monopoly.

Contrary to the view of many neoliberals, we find that the monetary reward conferred by IPRs is not the only motivation behind the pursuit of knowledge and innovation. There are individuals who pursue knowledge for its own sake or for the public good. This point is made forcefully in a recently published open letter on TRIPS that was signed by thirteen eminent scientists, all fellows of the Royal Society of Britain. They wrote: 'Patents are only one means for promoting discovery and invention. Scientific curiosity, coupled with the desire to benefit humanity, has been of far greater importance throughout history' (*Financial Times*, 14 February 2001: 20).

Neoliberals fail to acknowledge that in a great many industries private IPRs are not essential to the creation of new knowledge. In many industries, new technology cannot easily be replicated. This means that the innovator has something quite close to a monopoly on the new technology. It was on this basis that economist (and former Austrian finance minister) Joseph Schumpeter elaborated his theory of innovation. He argued that capitalist systems provide incentives for innovation because individuals can reap the rewards of innovation during a period of monopoly. Schumpeter did not envision a need for patents to create a period wherein the inventor holds a monopoly.

There is a case for *some* type of patent protection in cases where it is easy to replicate an innovator's technology. The chemical, pharmaceutical and software industries are examples of industries where replication of new technologies can be fairly easy. For this reason, these industries are among the most aggressive defenders of patentee rights. But protection of *some* patentee rights does not mean that the *unequivocal* protection that firms demand under the TRIPS agreement is appropriate.

Patents are sometimes of dubious use or legitimacy.

Many critics of the patent system argue that it encourages a 'winner-takes-all' mentality that leaves competitors racing for the next big find in some area. In this type of race, there is necessarily a good deal of duplicative effort and investment. This duplication of effort represents a waste of resources. Resources are wasted as well in efforts to sidestep existing patents in lieu of creating genuinely new knowledge. Critics of patents also argue that the patent system is inconsistent with the cumulative, interactive nature of technological progress. On this point, a group of critics observed that the 'strong protection of a key innovation may preclude the competitors from making socially useful innovation' (Levin et al. 1987: 788). Finally, critics have questioned the practice of granting all inventions an equal length of protection, and one that lasts as long as seventeen to twenty years in most countries.

Today, increasing attention is given to the problem of granting patents to certain inventions that rely upon ideas that are generated in publicly funded research activities. The story of the anti-AIDs drug, AZT, illustrates this problem (Palast 2000). AZT was invented in 1964 by a US researcher who was funded by a grant from the government's National Institute of Health (NIH). The UK pharmaceuticals company Glaxo then purchased the drug for use as a medication for pet cats. When the AIDS epidemic emerged, the NIH conducted research that demonstrated the usefulness of AZT on the HIV virus. Over the strenuous objections of the NIH, Glaxo lost no time in applying for a patent on AZT. Today, Glaxo reaps huge profits on AZT sales.

A final concern with patents is that they may now be hindering the advancement of knowledge. As increasingly minute pieces of knowledge become suitable for patent (say, down to the gene level), there is the risk that the pace of scientific progress will be slowed for administrative and financial reasons. The case of what is called golden rice (rice that has betacarotene inserted into it through genetic engineering) illuminates this dilemma. Golden rice has the potential to offer nutritional benefits to millions of people in the world. The two researchers that pioneered golden rice technology reported that they sold it to a TNC because of the difficulties involved in negotiating for the estimated 70–105 patents necessary for further development of the rice technology.[8]

> Patents were not important to the development of
> industrialized countries.

The historical record reveals that industrialized countries did not recognize or enforce patents until after the process of industrialization was complete. Switzerland introduced a patent law that protected mechanical inventions in 1888, but a comprehensive patent law was introduced only in 1907 (Schiff 1971). The Netherlands first introduced a patent law in 1817, but then abolished it in 1869 because patents were seen to create a monopoly that was inconsistent with the country's commitment to free trade and free markets (Schiff 1971). Patent law was reintroduced in the Netherlands only in 1912. Interestingly, the nineteenth-century economists that were most committed to free trade and free markets rejected patents because of the monopoly argument (Machlup and Penrose 1951).

Other industrialized countries had patent laws by the mid-nineteenth century. But until well into the twentieth century these laws fell well short of the stringent standards now demanded of developing countries through the TRIPS agreement. For instance, in the nineteenth century many countries granted patents to inventions that were imported from abroad, and generally did not check for originality prior to issuing a patent. Japan, Switzerland and Italy did not recognize patents on chemical and pharmaceutical substances (as opposed to the processes of creating them) until the 1970s. Canada and Spain did not recognize these types of patents until the early 1990s. Up until quite recently, India took the same approach to patents on chemical and pharmaceutical substances.

> Evidence shows that developing countries have yet to garner
> any rewards from TRIPS.

There is no reason to expect that TRIPS on their own can spur greater innovation in developing countries. There are many prerequisites for innovation (such as high levels of technical and scientific education) that are not presently met in developing countries.

There is very little evidence that TRIPS have encouraged technology transfer from industrialized to developing countries. In reality, TRIPS are more likely to reduce technology transfer and innovation. This is because TRIPS make it much more difficult for developing countries to adapt or imitate advanced technologies through reverse engineering or other informal channels of technology transfer (that involve minor modifications to a technology or the development of alternative processes for producing a patented substance). Historically, informal technology transfer has played an important role in developing countries. Unfortunately, the new TRIPS regime largely precludes it.

Finally, there is little evidence that protection of IPRs plays any role in foreign direct investment (FDI) decisions (see Chapter 9.4). Indeed, Switzerland's experience suggests the opposite: the absence of patent laws made the country attractive to foreign investors (Schiff 1971). Much the same has been shown for historical flows of FDI to Canada and Italy (UNDP 1999: 73). Some analysts have also noted that patents are often a substitute (and not a prerequisite) for FDI (Vaitsos 1972).

TRIPS have been costly to developing countries.

First, the most direct cost of TRIPS for developing countries is that large royalty payments must now be paid to corporations in industrialized countries. These royalty obligations compete with a range of existing demands on scarce foreign currency reserves.

Second, TRIPS have increased the power of TNCs vis-à-vis consumers. TRIPS make it more likely that TNCs will be able to engage in monopolistic behaviour, such as monopoly pricing. This is problematic since developing countries often have weak (and sometimes non-existent) anti-trust laws and/or weak enforcement capabilities, particularly in relation to foreign TNCs.

Third, a sophisticated regime of IPR protection requires large outlays of funds and the work of many sophisticated international patent lawyers and other technical advisers. This is especially clear when a country is involved in a TRIPS dispute within the WTO. Developing countries have many more pressing and socially important uses for their scarce resources and personnel.

Fourth, TRIPS have enabled firms in industrialized countries to patent many natural processes and resources that have always been readily available and unpatented in developing countries. This is largely due to the ability of firms in industrialized countries to repackage products and resources (even the most minute, such as micro-organisms and biological processes) that had long been a part of the traditional knowledge system in developing countries. Today, developing countries are in the position of paying foreign firms for the use of substances that had always been produced and available domestically. For instance, a US firm was prevented from acquiring a patent for the medicinal use of the spice turmeric only because the government of India – where such use was known for thousands of years – learned of the attempt and took the company to court.

Fifth and finally, TRIPS hamper certain forms of innovation and technological progress. TRIPS reduce the opportunities for incremental innovation in developing countries.

> It is not in the economic interest of developing countries to offer strong protection to IPRs.

IPRs are far less important in the promotion of innovation and technological advancement than neoliberals acknowledge. It is therefore in the economic interest of developing countries to maintain only weak protection of IPRs. Indeed, most developing countries are not at the point where IPRs are critical to the promotion of new technologies in the few industries where IPRs play some role in innovation. At this point, most developing countries are users rather than creators of new technology.

Patents and public interests – an illustration from the AIDS/HIV drug dispute

There has recently been a heated controversy over TRIPS. This concerns the dispute between pharmaceuticals companies in industrialized countries and their counterparts in developing countries (mainly Thailand, Brazil, India and Argentina). The latter sought to export inexpensive AIDS/HIV drugs to other developing countries, especially countries in sub-Saharan Africa.

Pharmaceuticals companies in industrialized countries sell these drugs for over twenty times their cost of production, even when the drugs are being sold to extremely poor countries. A few pharmaceuticals companies decided to offer very poor countries discounts on AIDS/HIV drugs following the public criticisms of their pricing practices. The companies made it abundantly clear that the discounts they offered were motivated by charitable concerns, and not by a change in their stance on IPRs. We know that the latter is true because these same companies were part of a coalition of forty-one pharmaceuticals companies that took the South African government to court in March 2001 on the grounds that its patent law grants the government too much power over patentee rights in the interests of public health. The companies claimed that the South African government's policy of compulsory licensing and parallel imports in the interests of public health are unconstitutional. Fortunately, an effective campaign by advocacy groups and much public outrage forced the pharmaceuticals companies to withdraw their lawsuit in return for a promise from the South African government that it will try to minimize the use of compulsory licensing.

Pharmaceuticals companies argue that they have no greater obligation to serve the public interest by providing subsidized medicine than food companies have to curb malnutrition by providing subsidized food (Pilling 2001). This argument is not compelling since the industry derives a large part of its profit from socially sanctioned monopolies (i.e. patents), on which the food industry does not rely to any comparable extent. Moreover, much research in the pharmaceuticals industry is actually financed by the public sector or private charities. Thus the industry has special obligations to the public that make it far different from other types of industry.

To conclude: excessive attention to patentee rights at the cost of broader human rights and public health leads to perverse outcomes. There are compelling reasons to dilute patentee rights in cases of public health crises. Governments in industrialized countries have disregarded patents in the name of public interest. Notably, the Canadian government overrode the patent of the Bayer Corporation on the medication Cipro during the anthrax scare in fall 2001. The threat of similar action by the US government enabled it to obtain a 50 per cent discount on the same medication.

Policy alternatives

> There are few economic benefits associated with enhanced protection of IPRs in developing countries.

Developing countries have an interest in the weak protection of IPRs. Alternative policy towards IPRs can take two paths: the spaces in the existing IPR regime can be exploited, and the regime itself can be challenged.

> Education and government support for targeted, applied research are much more important to the promotion of innovation in developing countries than are the protection of IPRs.

Far more important than the protection of IPRs is the promotion of innovation and technological progress in developing countries through other means. Efforts to promote innovation should be tightly linked to the goals of industrial policy (see Chapter 7.2). These objectives can be addressed through government support for education and other initiatives that might stimulate targeted types of research. Moreover, some reallocation of existing educational expenditures can free substantial resources for such initiatives. The government might also support some types of advanced education (even education abroad) in exchange for a period of public service.[9] The government might forgive a portion of any educational loan in exchange for a period of public service.

> Governments can use FDI as a strategic means to promote technology and knowledge transfers and to stimulate innovation by domestic researchers.

A strategic policy towards FDI can also promote technology transfer and innovation by domestic researchers. FDI can be a means of transferring technology if the government targets the attraction of some types of investment and structures operating agreements with this goal in mind (see Chapter 9.4). It is also possible to conceive of using FDI strategically to create partnerships between researchers in developing and industrialized countries. Indeed, some governments might negotiate research partnerships in FDI agreements. They might also negotiate research internships for some of their nationals in the corporation's research headquarters. This type of strategy might be especially useful for those countries that have a scant pool of well-trained researchers.

> Governments in developing countries should promote patents only in the few industries where they can be important in the generation of new knowledge.

As we have seen, patents can play a role in stimulating innovation in a few industries – namely, pharmaceuticals, chemicals and software. In these limited cases, governments may wish to pursue one of two strategies, depending on existing domestic R&D capabilities.

In countries with some existing R&D capabilities, the government can provide financial and administrative assistance to firms and university-based researchers that seek to patent their work. This assistance might be tied to the pursuit of research that contributes in some specific way to the attainment of industrial policy goals (see Chapter 7.2). The government might then share patent proceeds with the researchers that they fund. The government could also serve as a clearing house for some types of research. It might bring researchers together for strategic purposes or publicize potential applications of research that have not been patented.

In countries where existing R&D capabilities are minimal to non-existent, the government can organize and finance outside researchers to identify those aspects of traditional knowledge and local resources that can be patented. National or regional governments, local community organizations or government–private sector partners could hold patents developed through this approach.

> Governments in developing countries can use clauses within
> the existing TRIPS agreement to override some patents.

The success of developing countries in securing concessions on AIDS/HIV drugs (see above) suggests that this strategy can be used in the cases of other TRIPS. Foreign companies may grant other exceptions to TRIPS for reasons of public relations if developing countries press the case. It is worth pressing the clauses that speak to the public interest within the existing TRIPS agreement. Developing countries might pursue their challenges to TRIPS collectively in order to maximize their leverage and share the costs of advancing a case.

The existing TRIPS agreement provides for a grace period during which time developing countries are to move towards adoption of the IPR protections that prevail in industrialized countries. This grace period has expired for most developing countries, and will expire for the poorest of these in 2005. It is heartening that in the aftermath of the dispute over HIV/AIDS drugs, many supporters of TRIPS have suggested that the grace period be extended. It is critical that developing countries press forward on the matter of obtaining substantially longer and flexible grace periods for TRIPS.

The TRIPS regime should be challenged.

Finally, it is time to press for reconsideration of the entire TRIPS regime. The dilution of TRIPS and the expansion of the conditions under which exemptions are granted are particularly worthwhile directions for a new approach to TRIPS. Collective action on recasting the TRIPS regime is more than warranted at this time.

Notes

1. The case for privatization is primarily economic. However, it is also a matter of political (or even moral) value, as the freedom to acquire and dispose of private property is a core political and moral value of a free society.
2. Some statistical studies have found that the degree of competition faced by a firm – rather than its ownership structure – is an important factor in enterprise performance .
3. Following the 1996 privatization, the French state still controlled around 45 per cent of voting shares. Even after a major divestiture in 2002, the French state remained by far the greatest shareholder in the company (it owned about 35 per cent of voting shares).
4. The figures above are from Maddison 1989. The growth rates reported are between 1950 and 1987. The other two countries in the top seven of the growth league are Japan (6 per cent) and West Germany (3.8 per cent), economies where the state plays an active state role in economic activity, though SOE sectors are not large. The other nine economies in the study are, by descending order of growth rates, Belgium, Sweden, Denmark, the Netherlands, Switzerland, the UK, Australia, Canada and the USA.
5. In oil-producing countries, SOEs account for a very large proportion of national income, irrespective of the political orientation of the country's policymakers.
6. POSCO was privatized very recently.

7. Unfortunately, he did not believe that people were also like air as he owned slaves.
8. Some analysts of the golden rice story dispute the patent figure (RAFI 2000).
9. Enforcement is critical since many countries have these types of programme, but have not pressed recipients to honour their obligations to the country upon the completion of their education.

Policy Alternatives 3

International Private Capital Flows

9.1 **General Analysis**

Terminology

International capital flows consist of public and private flows. Public flows are capital transfers made between governments. This can take the form of bilateral flows, such as one government giving aid or lending money to another, or multilateral flows, such as lending from multilateral institutions like the IMF, the World Bank, the Asian Development Bank, and the Inter-American Development Bank.

International private capital flows consist of three main types: foreign bank lending, portfolio investment (PI) and foreign direct investment (FDI).[1] Foreign bank lending refers to the loans extended by commercial banks or multilateral institutions (such as the IMF and the World Bank) to domestic public- or private-sector borrowers. PI refers to the purchase of stocks, bonds, derivatives and other financial instruments issued by the private sector in a country other than one in which the purchaser resides. In the case of bonds, these can also be issued by the government and purchased by private investors. FDI refers to the purchase of a 'controlling interest' (defined as at least 10 per cent of the assets) in a business in a country other than one in which the investor resides. FDI can take two forms: 'greenfield' investment which involves the creation of a new facility – for example, the construction of a factory by a foreign investor; or 'brownfield' investment, namely mergers and acquisitions that involve the purchase of assets of existing domestic firms. The cross-border purchase of real estate is also classified as FDI.

Empirical trends

> The composition of international capital flows to developing countries shifted dramatically during the 1990s.

The 1990s witnessed pronounced changes in capital flows to developing countries. On the one hand, foreign aid flows stagnated as a consequence of changing political sentiments.[2] On the other hand, the composition of private capital flows shifted. Historically, foreign lending by commercial banks was the most significant type of private capital flow to developing countries. But during the 1990s, commercial banks curtailed this lending. The reduction in lending stemmed from two developments. Commercial banks became wary of lending to developing countries following the 'debt crisis' of the 1980s (though the largest banks were able to pass on the costs of these loans through various publicly financed initiatives). Banks also found the speculative opportunities available in the liberalized financial environment of the 1990s far more appealing than lending. The decline in both foreign lending and aid to developing countries in the 1990s elevated the importance of attracting FDI and PI flows, both of which increased significantly during this period.

These fundamental changes in the composition of international private capital flows to developing countries are illustrated in the following data (World Bank, various years).[3] The net flow of long-term bank lending (including bonds and excluding loans extended by the IMF) to developing countries was $US 7 billion in 1970, $65.3 billion in 1980, $43.1 billion in 1990, $5.1 billion in 2000, and –$9 billion in 2002.[4] Net FDI and PI flows to developing countries were scant until the 1990s, but grew dramatically thereafter. For example, net FDI to developing countries was $2.2 billion in 1970, $4.4 billion in 1980, $24.1 billion in 1990, $160.6 billion in 2000, and $143 billion in 2002. Net PI grew dramatically during the 1990s as well: it was zero in 1970 and 1980, $3.7 billion in 1990, $26 billion in 2000, and $9.4b in 2002. These latter data reveal tremendous volatility – a factor to which we return below.

> Despite the growth of PI and FDI to developing countries, their share of global flows is rather small and remains highly concentrated in large, middle-income countries.

The aggregate figures presented above illustrate key changes in the composition of international private capital flows to developing countries during the 1990s. However, these data do not reveal two important facts. The first is that developing countries receive a very small proportion of all global private capital flows. Even since 1990, the share of global PI flows that has gone to developing countries has remained rather low. Developing countries received just 9.7 per cent of global PI flows in 1991, 9.0 per cent in 1994, 6.2 per cent in 1998, and 5.5 per cent in 2000.[5] The second is that private capital flows are highly concentrated in a small number of middle-income, large developing countries. The World Bank (2003) reports that over the last thirteen years, the top eight developing countries have accounted for 84 per cent of total net flows of PI to the South. As with FDI, the largest net recipient of PI has been China, which has attracted 22 per cent of the developing country total since 1989. China is followed by Mexico, Brazil, South Africa, India, Thailand, Malaysia, and the Czech Republic. By contrast, the poorest countries receive very little of the PI flows that go to the developing world. In 2002, South Asian countries other than India (with 9.5 per cent of the developing world total) and sub-Saharan countries other than South Africa (with 7.4 per cent) received *no* net PI.

The picture for FDI is somewhat brighter: developing countries received 22.3 per cent of global FDI in 1991, 35.2 per cent in

1994, 25.9 per cent in 1998, and 15.9 per cent in 2000. FDI flows to developing countries are highly concentrated in roughly ten large, middle-income countries, however. During 1992–2001, the top ten recipients of FDI flows were (in descending order of importance) China, Brazil, Mexico, Argentina, Poland, Chile, Malaysia, Thailand, the Czech Republic and Venezuela. These ten countries received 70 per cent of the FDI flows that went to the developing world in 2002. By contrast, low-income developing countries receive a very small amount of private capital flows. (The World Bank defines low-income countries as those in which per capita gross national income in 2001 was $745 or less.) Low-income developing countries received just $0.3 billion of net FDI in 1970, $0.2 billion in 1980, $2.2 billion in 1990, $9.7 billion in 2000, and $7 billion in FDI in 2002; they received no PI in 1970 and 1980, $0.4 billion in 1990, $2.6 billion in 2000, and $2.5 billion in 2001.

Despite unevenness in the distribution of capital flows, and despite the small share of global capital flows that actually accrue to developing countries, neoliberals maintain that policy must target the attraction of these flows via the creation of open, liberalized markets (and other reforms). In sections 9.2, 9.3 and 9.4 of this chapter we discuss the specific claims and policies advanced by neoliberals as concerns each type of international private capital flow. Before doing so, let us review the general neoliberal case for the developmental benefits of unfettered capital flows.

The neoliberal view on international private capital flows

There are numerous economic benefits associated with unfettered international private capital flows.

Open capital markets give the public and the private sectors in developing countries access to capital and other resources (such as technology) that are not being generated domestically. Sufficient capital and other resources are not generated domestically because of low income, low savings and/or capital flight. Thus neoliberals maintain that an increase in private capital inflows will inaugurate a virtuous cycle by increasing the nation's capital stock, productivity and income. Sales of government bonds to foreign investors increase the resources available for public expenditure since these are rather scant thanks to problems with tax collection and the myriad demands on government budgets.

International private capital flows can also increase efficiency and policy discipline in developing countries. The need to attract private capital flows and the threat of capital flight (by domestic and/or foreign investors) are powerful incentives for the government and firms to maintain international standards for policy design, macroeconomic performance and corporate governance. For example, governments that seek to attract private capital flows will be more likely to pursue anti-inflationary economic policies (see Chapter 11.2 and 11.3) and anti-corruption measures because investors place a high value on price stability, transparency and the rule of law.

Moreover, the liberalization of international private capital flows means that these flows will be allocated by markets rather than by governments. This shift in the allocation mechanism increases efficiency and ensures that finance will be directed towards those projects that promise the greatest net contribution to social welfare. These, of course, will be the projects promising the highest rates of return.

For all of the reasons advanced above, the liberalization of capital flows is essential to the promotion of sound economic performance in developing countries, particularly with regard to investment, income and economic growth. Indeed, had the Asian financial crisis of 1997–98 not intervened, the IMF was poised to modify its Articles of Agreement to make the liberalization of all international private capital flows a central purpose of the Fund and to extend its jurisdiction to capital movements.

> While we should exercise a certain caution when it comes to liberalization of highly liquid international capital flows, the ultimate goal should be complete capital account liberalization.

A growing number of commentators argue that the liberalization of some types of capital flows should be undertaken only *after* successful liberalization of other sectors of the economy (such as the industrial sector), attainment of a minimal degree of financial development, and/or development of sufficient institutional and regulatory capacity. This is known as the 'sequencing' argument. However, this is not a universally accepted view. Many well-informed observers reject the case for sequencing and temporary capital controls on the grounds that they introduce problems (such as corruption, inertia in reform, slow growth, high capital costs) that are far worse than any financial instability associated with full-scale economic liberalization.

Advocates of sequencing generally find their case strengthened following financial crises, as these are seen as a consequence of premature financial liberalization. Notably, following the Asian crisis some studies (even some by IMF staff) have acknowledged that certain types of controls over international capital flows can prevent undue financial volatility in developing countries, *provided that* these controls are temporary and that the rest of the economy is liberalized (Prasad et al. 2003; Kuczynski and Williamson 2003).

It is important to recognize that even among advocates of sequencing there is no question that complete liberalization remains the *ultimate goal* for *all* developing countries.

Rejection of the general neoliberal view on international capital flows

There are numerous serious, general problems associated with unfettered international private capital flows.

All international private capital flows are associated – *albeit to different degrees and through different means* – with the following problems. Under a system of market-determined (termed 'floating') exchange rates, large, sudden inflows of capital can put pressure on the domestic currency to appreciate (see also section 9.3 and

Chapter 11.1). A large appreciation of the domestic currency is problematic because it can undermine the country's balance-of-payments position by causing imports to rise (as they become less expensive for domestic consumers) and exports to fall (as they become more expensive for consumers in other countries). Private capital inflows also increase the potential for domestic and foreign investors to have undue influence over domestic policy-making (as capital flows depend on investor judgements regarding the attractiveness of the economic and policy environment) and raise the spectre of excessive foreign control/ownership of domestic resources.

The flipside of capital inflows is, of course, the possibility of capital outflows (e.g. dividend payments to foreign investors, interest payments to foreign lenders, and the liquidation of stock portfolios). Sudden, large capital outflows (termed 'capital flight') can place pressure on the domestic currency to depreciate (see also section 9.3 below and Chapter 11.1). Capital flight often induces a vicious cycle of additional flight and currency depreciation, debt-service difficulties and reductions in stock (or other asset) values. This is because panicked investors tend to sell their assets en masse to avoid new capital losses brought about by anticipated future depreciations of currency or asset values. In this manner, capital flight introduces or aggravates existing macroeconomic vulnerabilities and financial instability. This can culminate in a financial crisis, an event that seriously compromises economic performance and living standards (particularly for the poor) and often provides a channel for undue foreign influence over domestic decision-making. Finally, markets are at least as apt as governments to allocate international capital flows in an inefficient, wasteful or developmentally unproductive manner (as we will see below).

> The case for liberalization of international capital flows is not supported by evidence.

Numerous recent cross-country and historical studies demonstrate conclusively that there is no reliable empirical relationship between the liberalization of capital flows and performance in terms of inflation, economic growth or investment in developing countries (e.g. Eichengreen 2001; Rodrik 1998). Moreover, there is now a large body of unambiguous empirical evidence that shows that the liberalization of international private capital flows introduces and/or aggravates important problems in developing countries. For example, numerous studies find that financial liberalization is strongly associated with banking, currency and financial crises (Demirgüc-Kunt and Detragiache 1998; Weller 2001). Other studies show that liberalization is associated with an increase in poverty and inequality (Weller and Hersh 2002).

> There is evidence from a variety of countries that well-designed capital controls have played an important role during crucial periods in the development process.

Capital controls refer to measures that manage the volume, composition or allocation of capital flows and/or maintenance of restrictions on investor entrance or exit opportunities. Nearly all industrialized countries utilized capital controls successfully over long periods. For example, Continental European countries employed extensive capital controls during the economic reconstruction that followed World War II. Even the USA – arguably the home of free capital flows, and also a country whose financial system has benefited importantly from the receipt of flight capital from around the world – used temporary capital controls in 1963 because they were warranted by economic circumstances.

Capital controls played critically important roles during the high-growth eras in Japan and South Korea and were successfully employed in Brazil in the 1950s and 1960s. Chile and Colombia successfully used capital controls during the 1990s. The Malaysian government successfully employed stringent capital controls in 1994 and 1998. Despite the fact that capital controls have fallen out of favour (as a consequence of the hegemony of neoliberal views), some economically successful countries such as China and India continue to employ extensive controls over a variety of investment and financial activities. Among these experiences, the capital controls in Chile and Colombia are the only ones that many neoliberals largely view in a positive light (see below).

Capital controls have the potential to achieve numerous objectives that policymakers have reason to value highly.

In this and the following chapter, we present evidence from a variety of countries to show that well-designed controls over various types of foreign and domestic capital flow can achieve important objectives. First, capital controls can promote financial stability and prevent the economic and social devastation that is associated with economic crises. Second, capital controls can promote desirable types of investment and financing arrangements (that is, investment/financing that is long-term, stable and sustainable, creates employment opportunities, improves living standards, promotes income equality, and encourages technology transfer and learning-by-doing) and discourage less desirable types of investment/financing strategies. Third, capital controls can enhance democracy and national autonomy by reducing the potential for speculators and various external actors to exercise undue influence over domestic decision-making and/or control over national resources.

General directions for alternative policies

International capital flows should be managed via capital controls.

Capital controls should target the specific vulnerabilities confronted by different economies. They can be maintained on a more or less permanent basis, or can be activated as warranted by economic conditions. The former type of control is far more common historically.

Under a system of vulnerability-activated controls, capital controls are utilized only when economic indicators reveal that they are warranted. In the approach developed by Grabel (2003a, 2004), graduated, transparent capital controls are activated whenever information about the economy indicates that controls are necessary to prevent nascent macroeconomic fragilities from culminating in serious difficulties or even in a crisis. There are two tools envisioned in this approach: 'trip wires' and 'speed bumps'. Trip wires are simple measures that warn policymakers and investors that a country is approaching high levels of risk in various domains (e.g. currency collapse, the flight of foreign lenders or investors, the emergence of fragile financing strategies, etc.). Once a trip wire predicts the emergence of a particular vulnerability, policymakers would then immediately take steps to curtail this risk by activating a targeted, graduated capital control, or what we call a speed bump.

Developing countries at different levels of wealth require distinct trip-wire thresholds. Trip wires would have to be appropriately sensitive to subtle changes in the risk environment and adjustable. Sensitive trip wires would allow policymakers to activate graduated speed bumps at the earliest sign of heightened risk, well before conditions for investor panic had materialized. Specific trip wires and speed bumps for foreign bank borrowing and PI are discussed in sections 9.2 and 9.3 below, respectively. The main rationale behind the trip wire–speed bump approach to capital controls is that it could slow unsustainable financing and investment patterns *before* they culminate in serious economic difficulties.

9.2 **Foreign Bank Borrowing**

The neoliberal view

> Foreign bank loans carry numerous macro- and microeconomic benefits.

The resources provided by foreign bank loans supplement the pool of capital that is made available by domestic lenders and savers. Foreign bank loans thereby provide the opportunity for levels of investment and economic growth that are higher than would otherwise be possible in the absence of this resource. Additionally, there are other developmental benefits associated with foreign bank borrowing. Foreign banks often extend credit at lower cost to borrowers than do domestic banks. These lower capital costs may translate into higher levels of investment and growth. The competition between foreign and domestic banks may also force the latter to offer loans at lower rates and more generally rise to the efficiency and service standards of their foreign competitors. Domestic consumers and firms thereby benefit from the competition between foreign and domestic banks.

Foreign bank borrowing also acts as a disciplining device on the macro- and micro-levels. On the macro-level, foreign bank borrowing rewards governments and firms for creating a sound financial environment and penalizes them for making poor choices (through the withdrawal of loans or the increase in interest rates). Foreign bank borrowing therefore reinforces the necessity for appropriate economic (and other) policy reforms. On the micro-level, the performance of domestic firms is enhanced by their relationship with foreign lenders. Domestic firms that borrow from foreign lenders must meet the stringent standards for creditworthiness and management competence that foreign banks impose on borrowers. By encouraging an upward harmonization of operating and management practices, foreign bank borrowing enhances economic efficiency in developing countries.

Rejection of the neoliberal view

A good deal of foreign bank borrowing has fuelled speculative bubbles and overinvestment, thus aggravating financial fragility.

The capital made available by foreign banks will only promote productive investment and economic growth if these funds are allocated appropriately (in a developmental sense). This has generally not been the case. In countries throughout the developing world, private borrowers use foreign bank loans to finance all manner of unproductive or wasteful activities.

During the speculative bubbles that are commonly inaugurated by financial liberalization, a large proportion of foreign bank loans finance forays into speculative commercial real estate development and stock trading (see section 9.3 below and Chapter 10). This was certainly the case in many Latin American and Southeast Asian countries following financial liberalization. In addition to providing fuel for speculative bubbles, foreign bank borrowing has often financed investment in sectors where there is substantial overcapacity. In the years leading up to the Asian financial crisis, foreign loans financed a good deal of overinvestment (e.g. in the production of automobiles and electronics). Excess capacity (which is the outcome of overinvestment) places downward pressure on prices and export earnings.

In the absence of government measures that influence the allocation of loan proceeds, there is no reason to expect that foreign loans will finance investment projects of the highest developmental or social value. It hardly matters if foreign loans complement the scant volume of domestic loans if these loans are used for developmentally unproductive purposes. Neoliberals are certainly correct in their claim that foreign loans are often cheaper than loans extended by domestic lenders. But the lower cost of foreign lending is of dubious developmental benefit if this makes the use of these funds for unproductive purposes more attractive, which it often does.

Foreign loans are also associated with the introduction and/or aggravation of problems of maturity and locational mismatch. Maturity mismatch refers to the situation wherein long-term investments are financed with short-term loans. This makes borrowers vulnerable to changes in the price and availability of short-term credit whenever they seek renewed financing. Foreign banks often offer short-term loans at very attractive prices, something that credit-constrained borrowers in developing countries find advantageous. But severe financial difficulties are created later when local borrowers find it difficult or costly to 'roll over' their short-term debt for new debt. Locational mismatch refers to the situation wherein foreign debts must be repaid in a currency other than the borrowers' own national currency. Locational mismatch is the norm in developing countries since the vast majority of foreign loans must be repaid in 'hard currencies' such as the US dollar, the yen or the euro. Locational mismatch renders borrowers in developing countries vulnerable to depreciations of their own currency since this raises the cost of debt service. Both maturity and locational mismatch played important roles in the recent financial crises in Mexico, East Asia and Argentina.

Foreign loans are more prone to flight risk than are domestic loans. Foreign lenders are more apt to curtail their lending in a particular country to protect themselves from perceived risks or to pursue better opportunities elsewhere. Not least, this is because governments in developing countries are not able to influence the decisions of foreign lenders in the same way that they might be able to influence domestic banks through policy directives or moral suasion. A sudden withdrawal of foreign lending can trigger or exacerbate financial instability, as was evident in many East Asian countries in 1997–98 and in Argentina in 2001–02.

> There is a powerful reward and penalty function to foreign bank borrowing. This, of course, hardly recommends it.

Neoliberals are certainly correct in their assertion that foreign loans provide incentives and rewards to governments and firms that pursue (what they view as) 'appropriate' courses of action (and likewise discourage or penalize inappropriate courses). Given the prevailing ideological climate, foreign bank borrowing therefore reinforces the necessity to pursue the neoliberal course and no other. Quite apart from the inappropriateness of neoliberal policies, it is rather surprising that neoliberals fail to acknowledge sufficiently that the allocation of foreign loans (and the decision to forgive them in case of default) is often highly politicized. Since the dawn of foreign lending, geopolitics has often played at least as important a role as objective economic analysis in determining the allocation and terms of bank lending to developing countries.

> Foreign bank lending does not force domestic banks to lower capital costs or enhance their efficiency.

There is no unambiguous evidence that competition between foreign and domestic lenders forces the latter to lower capital costs. This is because domestic and foreign lenders do not serve the same markets within developing countries, and therefore do not actually compete with one another. Foreign banks generally extend credit to larger firms (especially to larger firms that have ties to international markets), leaving small and medium-size firms dependent on domestic banks. In addition, although domestic banks themselves are often customers of foreign banks, this does not generally translate into easier credit for small borrowers. Especially during speculative booms, domestic banks often obtain loans from foreign banks that they use to participate in speculative opportunities.

On its own, interaction between foreign and domestic lenders does not result in the transfer of superior operating practices and efficiency standards. A carefully structured joint-operating agreement might accomplish this aim, but this objective often proves to be elusive. Foreign lenders exercise poor judgement and weak oversight during speculative booms to no less an extent than domestic lenders. The aftermath of recent financial crises in developing countries reveals quite clearly that foreign banks were parties to as much 'irrational exuberance' as were domestic banks. Indeed, many of the recent speculative bubbles in developing countries would likely not have grown so precipitously in the absence of the participation of foreign lenders.

> The burdens of servicing foreign debt can be devastating.

Foreign borrowing has saddled countries throughout the developing world with a vast 'debt overhang' that results in huge resource transfers from debtor to creditor countries. These debt burdens have frustrated the prospects for long-term economic growth, have wrought misery and social devastation, and have sacrificed the aspirations of the majority of the population in the developing world to the imperative of debt service. The pressure to service foreign debt has also encouraged environmental degradation as natural resources are often depleted in a race to earn scarce foreign exchange. The IMF structural adjustment programmes that so often accompany debt crises have induced vast economic and social dislocation in many regions of the developing world. Finally, the conditions attached to foreign loans, especially by the IMF, erode domestic policy autonomy and even hijack democracy.

Policy alternatives

There are several ways to manage the permissible level of foreign debt.

It is critical that developing countries drastically reduce their reliance on foreign bank loans. These countries will clearly gain by reducing the permissible volume of foreign bank loans. It would therefore be of significant benefit if policymakers enforced strict ceilings on the volume of new foreign loans that can be incurred. Such ceilings might involve strict limits on the allowable ratio of foreign to total loans, or might require that firms finance only a certain percentage of their projects with foreign loans that have a certain maturity and/or locational profile.

Restrictions on foreign borrowing could be deployed dynamically as circumstances warrant, following the trip wire–speed bump approach (see section 9.1 above). Under this approach, policymakers would monitor a trip wire that measures the economy's vulnerability to the cessation of foreign lending. This involves calculating the ratio of the government's holdings of currency reserves to private and public foreign-currency-denominated debt (with short-term obligations receiving a greater weight in the calculation). If this ratio approached an announced threshold, policymakers would then activate a graduated speed bump that precluded new inflows of foreign loans until circumstances improved.

> Policy can also discourage – rather than prohibit – the use of foreign loans as a source of finance.

The tax system can be used in a number of ways to discourage domestic borrowers from incurring foreign debt obligations. Domestic borrowers might pay a fee to the government or the central bank equal to a certain percentage of any foreign loan undertaken. This surcharge might vary based on the structure of the loan, such that loans that involve a locational or maturity mismatch incur a higher surcharge. Alternatively, the surcharge might vary based on the level of indebtedness of the particular borrower involved, such that borrowers who already hold large foreign debt obligations face higher surcharges than do less indebted borrowers. This tax-based approach could encourage borrowers to use domestic sources of finance since these would not carry any surcharge. Another strategy might involve varying the surcharge according to the type of activity that was being financed by foreign loans. For instance, borrowers might be eligible for a partial rebate on foreign loan surcharges when loans are used to finance export-oriented production.

Note that policymakers in Chile and Colombia employed tax-based policies to discourage foreign borrowing during much of the 1990s. In Chile, foreign loans faced a tax of 1.2 per cent per year (payable by the borrower). Chilean policymakers also imposed a non-interest-bearing reserve requirement of 30 per cent on all types of foreign debts (and, indeed, on all foreign financial investments in the country). This policy, termed the reserve requirement tax, was in place from May 1992 to October 1998. The required reserves held against foreign obligations (and payable by the borrower) were kept at the central bank for one year, regardless of the maturity of the obligation. Authorities in Colombia also employed a reserve requirement tax specifically designed to discourage domestic borrowers from incurring foreign loans.

Beginning in September 1993, Colombian policymakers required that non-interest-bearing reserves of 47 per cent be held for one year against foreign loans with maturities of eighteen months or less (this was extended to loans with a maturity of up to five years in August 1994).[6] In addition, foreign borrowing related to real estate transactions was prohibited. Empirical studies of Chilean and Colombian policies conclude that they achieved their principal objectives, including the reduction in foreign borrowing (see Grabel 2003a, and references therein).

> To the extent that borrowers assume at least some foreign loan obligations, it is imperative that the allocation and terms of these loans be managed by the government.

Careful management of the allocation of foreign debt can ensure that it is used for productive, developmental purposes. Prior to financial liberalization in the 1990s, many governments in East and Southeast Asia tightly coordinated allocation and access to foreign loans. Policymakers in China and India today continue such practices (for details, see Epstein et al. 2003). For example, domestic Chinese firms must obtain government approval for any foreign borrowing undertaken. Though the Indian government has been steadily liberalizing the financial sector during the 1990s, it nevertheless maintains strict restrictions over the level and terms of the external debts held by domestic firms. Responding to the lessons of the 1997 Asian crisis, India continues to restrict commercial borrowing in foreign currencies. The Ministry of Finance maintains annual ceilings on the size and interest rate on loans sought by domestic firms. The Ministry also rules on requests for foreign borrowing on a case-by-case basis, making this determination based on the maturity structure and end-use of the proposed loan. In the approval process, priority is given to longer-term loans and to loans for priority sectors. Firms in China and India have low levels of external indebtedness and external financial fragility precisely because of government policies towards external debt.

In general, policymakers should implement measures that restrict or otherwise discourage domestic borrowers from using financing strategies that involve locational and maturity mismatch. In addition to the ceilings, surcharges and approval processes discussed above, policymakers can design trip wires and speed bumps that are designed to keep the levels of maturity and/or locational mismatch below the critical thresholds. A trip wire for locational mismatch is the ratio of foreign-currency-denominated debt to domestic-currency-denominated debt (with short-term obligations receiving a greater weight in the calculation). A trip wire for maturity mismatch is the ratio of short-term debt to long-term debt (with foreign-currency-denominated obligations receiving a greater weight in the calculation). A graduated series of speed bumps that require borrowers to reduce their extent of locational or maturity mismatch would be implemented whenever trip wires revealed the early emergence of these vulnerabilities.

> Economic reforms could replace the resources initially lost
> by the reduction in foreign borrowing due to debt ceilings,
> surcharges or speed bumps.

Critics may counter that economic growth will come to a standstill if access to foreign loans (or any other type of capital inflow) is restricted. However, reforms that are supposed to be friendly to foreign investors often result in a collapse of investment. For example, after the financial crisis in Korea, neoliberal financial reform made the country far more open to foreign capital inflows. However, these reforms did not lead to an increase in investment. Instead, the average investment ratio in GDP in Korea fell from 37.1 per cent during 1990–97 to 25.9 per cent during 1998–2002.

By contrast, governments that take steps to restrict foreign borrowing can replace at least some of the finance that is forgone by implementing measures that increase the pool of domestic finance. In this connection, measures that restrict the exit options of domestic savers and businesses would increase the pool of capital available domestically (since so much of it is presently lost to capital flight; see section 9.3 below and Chapter 10). The coordination of industrial policy and domestic financial regulation can also ensure that domestic firms have access to capital that is generated domestically (see Chapters 7.2 and 10). Tax reform is yet another means of increasing the domestic resource base (see Chapter 11.3). More generally, many of the economic policy reforms discussed in Part II are intended to generate higher levels of investment and economic growth. If these reforms are success-ful, the economy in the medium to long term will generate new resources that can be used to finance additional investment.

9.3 **Portfolio Investment**

The neoliberal view

> PI confers even greater rewards than other forms of foreign capital on recipient countries.

Portfolio investment (PI) gives firms and governments access to the vast pool of capital available on global financial markets. Increased access to capital inaugurates a virtuous cycle of increased investment and economic growth. PI is competitively priced and efficiently allocated by diverse and dispersed investors in global capital markets. Access to PI enhances the economy's overall ef-ficiency and performance. This is because the global capital markets through which PI is allocated utilize 'arm's-length' or non-relational practices that are not prone to corruption (as are government-based allocations of capital and some types of bank lending), and these markets are characterized by rapid price adjustment. The revers-ibility of PI promotes discipline and efficiency on the part of governments and firms in so far as their access to capital depends on investor confidence in their operating practices.

Though all of these benefits are associated with foreign bank borrowing (see section 9.2 above), they obtain to a more significant degree in the case of PI because the potential pool of capital is both greater and more liquid. Thus, not only does PI have more potential to promote economic growth, but it also has greater potential to serve a reward–penalty function (due to its liquidity). Additionally, PI promotes the diffusion of risk (and thereby financial stability and investment) through the wide dispersal of asset ownership on capital markets. Finally, PI is superior to foreign bank borrowing because the former is associated neither with conditionality nor with external control.

Rejection of the neoliberal view

Unregulated PI is not conducive to development and creates or aggravates important problems.

There is no empirical support for the argument that PI induces a virtuous cycle of investment and growth. As with foreign bank borrowing (see section 9.2 above), there is no compelling reason to believe that PI will necessarily be used to finance investment projects of the greatest developmental importance.

In contrast to financial flows that are mediated by governments, PI is allocated on global capital markets in accordance with rate-of-return criteria. In practice, this means that speculative projects (such as commercial real estate development) are more likely to receive capital than are projects with a high social or developmental return (such as the construction of roads). These speculative projects are often profitable to a small group of domestic and/or foreign investors and can increase investment and growth in the short and medium term. But speculation in PI contributes little to broader economic development and often aggravates inequality.

A high volume of unregulated PI can also increase macro-economic instability. In a great many developing countries, the collapse of speculative bubbles in the stock market contributed significantly to financial crises (e.g. Mexico in 1994–95, Malaysia and Thailand in 1997). Evidence shows that financial crises have serious, lasting economic and social costs, the burdens of which are borne disproportionately by the poor. Studies find that crises have been followed by increases in poverty rates and income inequality and by reductions in the rate of economic growth (Weller and Hersh 2002, and references therein).

PI is not inherently superior to other forms of finance.

The neoliberal claim that PI is superior to other forms of finance (particularly domestic bank borrowing) is incorrect. Portfolio investors are often diverse and dispersed. But these attributes are not necessarily conducive to development. The historical record shows that development success is often associated with *committed* – rather than disinterested – investors. This was the case during high growth eras in Continental Europe, Japan, East Asia and Latin America. Even in the USA – a country commonly seen to epitomize arm's-length investment practices – economic development until the Second World War was fostered by relational finance of various sorts, such as investment consortia, public–private partnerships, and even practices that would now be termed 'insider trading'.

> The rapid price adjustment associated with PI increases economic uncertainty and aggravates financial fragility. Liquidity also exacerbates problems relating to the exchange rate, international trade, financial instability and living standards.

Neoliberals are also correct in their claim that the global capital markets that allocate PI are characterized by a rapid (almost instantaneous) price adjustment mechanism. This is hardly a benefit, as asset price volatility increases uncertainty within particular firms (as managers cannot be certain about the cost of obtaining finance at a future time), induces systemic instability, and can thereby create a vulnerability to financial crisis. Price adjustments on capital markets are driven as much (if not more) by investor whim and market psychology as by careful, scientific evaluation of investment prospects.

PI is highly liquid and hence easily reversible. The sudden exit of a significant quantity of PI (held by either domestic or foreign investors) can and has induced a vicious cycle of additional flight and currency depreciation, debt-service difficulties and asset price deflation. As events in East Asia in 1997 make clear, this type of vicious cycle can culminate in a costly and painful national financial crisis. As mentioned earlier, the human costs of financial crises are disproportionately borne by the poor. Financial crises can be stimulated by the flight of any type of capital, but the high liquidity of PI renders it particularly prone to flight. (This is not to say that foreign direct investment is unproblematic or homogenous; see section 9.4 above.)

It is important to note that capital flight by domestic portfolio investors is as problematic as the exit of foreigners, even though the latter are often cast as villains in financial crisis scenarios. Indeed, domestic investors sometimes exit earlier than foreign investors because they are more aware of problems in their own economies. Capital flight by domestic investors is problematic not just because of its contribution to financial instability, but also because it increases the importance of attracting foreign investment as an alternative source of financing and decreases the domestic tax base (on the latter issue, see Chapter 11.3).

Large, sudden outflows of PI are not the only problem. Large, sudden inflows of PI are also problematic in so far as they can place the domestic currency under pressure to appreciate if exchange rates are market determined (see Chapter 11.1). In this case, a country's success in attracting large volumes of PI over a short period of time can threaten its export performance. Note that the same problem is introduced whenever large FDI inflows come in over a very short period of time – for example, when foreign investors purchase the majority of assets of several large domestic corporations.[7] If the exchange rate is fixed or pegged within some band, a large volume of portfolio or some types of FDI inflows can nevertheless tax the resources of domestic monetary authorities as they struggle to maintain the exchange rate within a predetermined range.

> PI introduces powerful, albeit indirect, constraints on policy autonomy.

Neoliberals celebrate the disciplining effect of PI on governments. We see the matter quite differently. The constraints on policy autonomy associated with PI frequently exact a powerful toll on developing economies, particularly with regard to growth and living standards (Grabel 1996).

Governments may be hesitant to consider policies that might displease domestic or foreign portfolio investors because they fear that such policies will trigger a large-scale investor exit. Portfolio investors have a particular dislike for any policy that they believe will induce or aggravate inflation because this reduces the rate of return on their investment. In the neoliberal view, government expenditure (especially when it is deficit-financed) triggers inflation. (See Chapter 11.3 for a critique of the expenditure–deficit–inflation nexus.) The perceived (though incorrect) link between government expenditure and inflation means that expansionary spending programmes become harder to justify once policymakers seek to attract PI at all costs. Expansionary monetary policy (i.e. policy that results in a reduction in domestic interest rates) is viewed in a similarly problematic light because neoliberals see it as a catalyst for increased spending, inflation and decreased economic growth (see Chapter 11.2 for a critique of this view). It also becomes more difficult for governments to enact any policies that restrict investor freedom because these too are seen to discourage PI. The range of constraints on policy autonomy described here are obviously indirect, but they are no less powerful for their subtlety.

Note that financial crises introduce severe and direct constraints on policy autonomy. In a crisis environment, drastic expenditure reductions and interest rate increases are often seen as necessary to restore the confidence (and induce the return) of portfolio investors. The IMF continues to press contractionary fiscal and monetary policy on developing countries when they are in crisis despite the fact that empirical evidence suggests that this strategy does not work. Contractionary policy failed to convince portfolio investors to return to South Korea and Argentina following their recent financial crises, as these policies increased bankruptcy rates and exacerbated overall risks in the economy. Notwithstanding this evidence, many neoliberals maintain that restoration of investor confidence necessitates contractionary policy at precisely the time when a more expansionary policy is needed to promote economic recovery and protect vulnerable social groups.

Policy alternatives

> Controls over PI warrant serious consideration. These controls have contributed importantly to economic development in a range of countries.

Careful management of PI can maximize the benefits and minimize the costs associated with this resource. Many countries successfully regulated PI for extended periods of time. For instance, during the two decades that followed World War II all industrialized countries heavily regulated PI inflows and outflows (Helleiner 1994). The only exception was the USA, but even it resorted to temporary controls over PI for a short time in the 1960s when policymakers sought to enhance confidence in the country's faltering economy. Indeed, most Continental European countries and Japan maintained stringent controls over portfolio and other capital flows until the mid-1980s.

The use of capital controls was not confined to industrialized countries. Controls over PI were the norm in developing countries until neoliberal economic reforms attained the status of orthodoxy. By any reasonable account, controls over portfolio and other capital flows contributed importantly to the success of numerous developing countries during the era of their strongest economic performance, namely the period between the 1950s and the mid-1970s. Compared to the neoliberal era, developing countries as a whole witnessed impressive economic performance during the three decades that followed World War II, a time when capital controls were used rather widely (see Chapter 1). Controls over capital movements (in addition to industrial and trade policy) contributed significantly to the strong economic performance of many East and Southeast Asian countries during the 1970s and 1980s (see Chapters 5 and 7).

> Some developing countries continue to use (or have recently used) controls over PI in the service of important objectives.

Even in the current neoliberal climate, a few large developing countries have effectively utilized controls over PI inflows and outflows. Here we identify some recent examples of such strategies (for additional examples, see Grabel 2003a and Epstein et al. 2003).

Malaysian authorities twice imposed restrictions over PI during the current neoliberal era. The first such effort was in early 1994. At that time, the Malaysian economy received dramatic increases in the volume of private capital inflows (including, but not limited to, PI). Policymakers were concerned that these inflows were feeding an unsustainable speculative boom in real estate and stock prices and were creating pressures on the domestic currency. In this context, policymakers implemented stringent, temporary inflow controls. These measures included restrictions on the maintenance of domestic-currency-denominated deposits and borrowing by foreign banks, controls on the foreign exchange exposure of domestic banks and large firms, and prohibitions on the sale to foreigners of domestic money market securities with a maturity of less than one year.

Reaction to these measures was rapid and dramatic, so much so that authorities were able to dismantle them as planned in under a year (as they achieved their goals during this time). During the period that the controls were in place, the volume of net private capital inflows and short-term inflows fell sharply, the composition of these flows was altered significantly, pressure on the currency was reduced, and the inflation of stock and real estate prices was curtailed (Palma 2000). The immediate, powerful reaction to these temporary controls underscores the potential of speed bumps to stem incipient difficulties successfully (see below).

The Malaysian government again implemented stringent controls over capital inflows and outflows in 1998 during the Asian financial crisis. This effort involved restrictions on foreign access to the domestic currency, on international transfer and trading of the currency, and on the convertibility of currency held outside the country. The government also established a fixed value for the domestic currency, closed the secondary market in equities, and prohibited non-residents from selling local equities held for less than one year.

By numerous accounts, these rather stringent measures prevented the further financial implosion of the country – a notable achievement since the country was also gripped by a severe political and social crisis during this time. Comparing the situation of Malaysia to other countries that were party to the Asian crisis, studies find that the country's capital controls were responsible for the faster recovery of its economy and stock market as well as the smaller reductions in employment and wages (Kaplan and Rodrik 2001). The latter achievements were possible because capital controls provided the government with the ability to implement reflationary economic and social policies uninhibited by the threat of additional capital flight or IMF disapproval.

From 1992 to 1998, policymakers in Chile and Colombia regulated PI rather extensively and successfully. During that time, the Colombian government did not allow foreign investors to purchase debt instruments or corporate equity. This policy was designed to prevent the possibility that financial instability could be induced by the sudden exit of foreign investors from liquid investment holdings. However, there were no significant controls on FDI. The differential treatment of FDI and PI was intended to promote the type of foreign investment that the government deemed important to economic growth, while protecting the economy from destabilizing forms of investment.

The Chilean government had similar motivations for its policy towards foreign investment in the country. By using the reserve requirement tax of 30 per cent on foreign investment, the government sought to lengthen the time horizon of investment and encourage more stable forms of foreign investment (see section 9.2 above). FDI and PI faced a one-year residence requirement. The government also prevented pension fund managers from investing more than 12 per cent of their assets abroad. This policy was intended to curb the possibility of capital flight by the most important type of large domestic investor.

Numerous empirical studies conclude that financial controls in Chile and Colombia played a constructive role in changing the composition and maturity structure (though not the volume) of net capital inflows, particularly after the controls were strengthened in 1994–95 (see Grabel 2003a, and references therein). Following implementation of these policies in both countries, external financing in general moved from debt to FDI. Policymakers in both Chile and Colombia were able to implement growth-oriented policies because the risk of foreign investor flight was significantly curtailed by their financial controls. Finally, the macroeconomic stability fostered by these financial controls contributed to the financial stability experienced by Chile and Colombia following the Mexican and the Asian financial crises. For instance, while other countries in Latin America were devastated by these events (due to the exit of investors from equity and government bond markets), Chile remained largely stable and only began to experience a significant reduction in private capital inflows in August 1998.

In the case of China, the participation of foreigners in equity markets is tightly limited, and the activities of its largely state-owned banks remain tightly circumscribed (e.g. lending to foreigners is precluded and access to foreign currency is restricted). Chinese residents also face substantial obstacles to capital expatriation. In fact, the Chinese government tightened existing restrictions and introduced new controls over finance following the Asian crisis. As the crisis unfolded, the Chinese government announced new restrictions on foreign exchange transactions involving more than $100,000, introduced new measures making it more difficult for domestic and international companies to move money into and out of the country, and introduced strict new penalties on Chinese companies that maintained illegal foreign currency deposits overseas. Similarly, during the Asian financial crisis, Taiwanese authorities also took steps to prevent illegal trading of funds managed by George Soros (because these funds were blamed for causing the local stock market to fall).

> There is a strong case for restricting the access of domestic investors to foreign capital markets.

The flight of domestic investors can induce financial instability and other economic problems, such as reductions in the tax base. For these reasons, there is a strong case for restricting the ability of domestic investors to hold foreign savings accounts and engage in capital flight.

In the mid-1980s, despite being the fourth largest foreign debtor in the world, Korea was saved from a debt crisis partly because of draconian controls on capital outflows. China and India provide more recent examples. China maintains stringent restrictions on the ability of domestic investors to engage in foreign PI (by limiting their access to foreign currencies in the first place). India, too, maintains firm controls over the exit options of domestic investors by restricting their access to foreign currency. Indian residents and firms are simply precluded from maintaining foreign currency accounts abroad, and Indian banks cannot accept deposits or extend loans in foreign currencies. Recent studies have shown that the combined effects of restrictions on capital flight, currency speculation, and access to foreign currency and loans protected China and India from instability during the Asian financial crisis.

Strategies for managing PI.

The discussion above suggests that there are several directions for managing PI. The success of blunt restrictions on PI in China, India, Chile and Colombia suggests that foreign investors do not necessarily shun countries with minimum-stay requirements on foreign investment or other financial controls. We have also seen that the tax system can be used to influence the composition and/or maturity structure of international capital flows. The potential for flight by domestic investors and savers can be reduced via implementation of exit taxes, prohibitions on flight, or restrictions on access to foreign currencies. Finally, Malaysian experience suggests that temporary controls on PI can be effective as well.

The trip wire–speed bump approach lends itself to the design of temporary controls over PI (see section 9.1 above). A trip wire that would reveal the vulnerability to PI flight risk is the ratio of total accumulated foreign PI to gross equity market capitalization or gross domestic capital formation. If the trip wire revealed that a country was particularly vulnerable to the reversal of PI inflows, a graduated series of speed bumps would slow the entrance of new inflows until the ratio falls either because domestic capital formation or gross equity market capitalization increased sufficiently or because foreign PI falls. Thus a speed bump on PI would slow unsustainable financing patterns until a larger proportion of any increase in investment could be financed domestically. We emphasize the importance of speed bumps governing *inflows* of PI because they exert their effects at times when the economy is attractive to foreign investors, and so are not as likely as outflow restrictions to trigger investor panic. Though not a substitute for outflow controls, inflow restrictions also reduce the frequency with which they must be used, and their magnitude.

It bears mentioning that one type of PI is not amenable to the trip wire–speed bump approach. The risks introduced by what are termed off-balance-sheet activities, such as derivatives, cannot be revealed by trip wires and hence cannot be curbed by speed bumps. This is because firms are not required to report data on off-balance-sheet activities (on their balance sheets). The risks of off-balance-sheet activities are far from trivial. Several studies demonstrate the significant role played by off-balance-sheet activities in the Asian financial crisis (Dodd 2000).

Trip wires and speed bumps for off-balance-sheet activities could be designed if policymakers compel actors to make these activities transparent through the imposition of reporting requirements. In the absence of the will to enforce transparency, policymakers in developing countries would be well advised to forbid domestic actors from engaging in off-balance-sheet activities. The Indian government wisely maintains stringent restrictions over transactions in derivatives.

9.4 **Foreign Direct Investment**

The neoliberal view

Foreign direct investment (FDI) is beneficial to developing countries because it provides them with access to capital and advanced technologies, introduces superior managerial techniques and business practices, and provides links with and access to foreign markets.

FDI and other transnational corporation activities (such as technology licensing and providing contract management without investment) promote the integration of developing countries into the global economy. FDI is a 'win–win' proposition for developing countries. What is good for the TNCs that undertake these investments is also good for the economies that host them.

The restrictive policies towards TNCs that were popular in developing countries in the 1960s and 1970s are products of misguided ideologies. In the words of a prominent business economist, '[i]t is no longer appropriate to assume that government and corporate objectives conflict' (Julius 1994: 278). In this connection, the former British European Commissioner Leon Brittan is correct to note that it is fortunate today that '[i]nvestment is recognized for what it is: a source of extra capital, a contribution to a healthy external balance, a basis for increased productivity, additional employment, effective competition, rational production, technology transfer, and a source of managerial knowhow' (Brittan 1995: 2).

> FDI has always been important to economic development. But its importance is greater now thanks to the globalization of production and corporate organization.

During the last two decades, international trade, production processes and corporate organization have all undergone dramatic transformation. The combined effect of these changes renders attraction of FDI all the more important to developing countries.

Up until the 1980s, the production process for a single commodity took place mostly within the confines of a single country (though necessary technology and/or raw materials may have been imported). 'Traditional' international trade consisted of trade in goods produced within the confines of a single nation. Since the 1980s, the production process has been broken down into numerous tasks, many of which are dispersed globally in what has been variously termed a global production web, global production network, global value chain, and global assembly line. If developing countries are to benefit from the newly emerging patterns of international production and trade, they must secure a place in the global production web.

Corporations have also changed during the last two decades. They are no longer associated with a particular nation. National corporations are increasingly becoming transnational or 'stateless'. Increasingly, core corporate activities (such as R&D) and even the corporate headquarters of TNCs are located outside the traditional home of what were formerly national corporations. The emergence of what is termed a world car or a global car and the establishment of R&D centres in the USA or Europe by Japanese- or Korean-owned computer firms exemplify the new form of corporate organization. The stateless nature of today's corporations helps to explain their positive-sum effects on developing countries. TNCs have no reason to exploit their host economies because the corporations have no national interest.

Data bear out the importance of these changes in trade patterns, production processes and corporate organization. Since 1982, FDI has been growing about four times faster than (traditional) international trade. Since the 1970s, the combined output of TNCs has exceeded the volume of international trade. The recent massive increase in FDI flows to developing countries suggests that a greater number of countries are being drawn into the global production web. About 75 per cent of all world trade in manufactured goods is conducted through TNCs, and well over a third of this activity is intra-firm (in addition to inter-country) trade.

> FDI is superior to all other forms of international private capital flows.

The stability of FDI renders it far preferable to foreign bank borrowing and PI. Its stability is particularly important, given the recent increases in financial instability and the crises that have been associated with the sudden reversal of liquid, volatile flows of foreign bank loans and PI.

> Countries that have unconditionally welcomed FDI have performed impressively.

The historical and empirical record shows that several countries have reaped the benefits of a liberal stance towards FDI and other forms of TNC involvement. The East Asian 'miracle' economies and some Latin American countries over the last two decades (particularly Mexico) are examples of the way that an open attitude towards FDI (and other TNC activities, as well as to international trade) can promote industrial development, export success, and growth.

> Countries that restrict FDI or the activities of TNCs will suffer from isolation or capital flight.

TNCs will not locate in countries that restrict their activities, and will exit countries that initiate restrictions on existing TNCs. The creation of global production networks and the increased liberalization of FDI policies across the world have made it easy for TNCs to relocate any aspect of the production process if the climate in the host country becomes hostile. As we have seen (in sections 9.2 and 9.3 above), the threat of exit can keep government policy towards FDI and TNCs in line with appropriate international standards of openness.

Rejection of the neoliberal view

> Historically, FDI and other TNC activities have been associated with numerous problems in the developing world. These problems have not disappeared.

In the 1960s and 1970s critics advanced many arguments against FDI and the activities of TNCs in developing countries. First, critics argued that TNCs transferred obsolete and 'inappropriate' technology to developing countries, often at inflated prices. Second, TNCs exercised enormous monopoly power over political and economic conditions within host economies. Third, TNCs evaded taxes by engaging in the practice of 'transfer pricing' between their subsidiaries. (Transfer pricing refers to a tax strategy that involves manipulating the 'internal prices' between subsidiaries of the same firm so that profits are recorded in countries that maintain lower taxes on foreign firms, and losses are recorded in countries that maintain higher taxes.) Fourth, TNCs discouraged domestic investment because local firms could not compete with foreign firms. In some instances, TNCs were criticized for their involvement in campaigns to destabilize governments that were unfriendly to their interests. The most famous such example involved the support by TNCs in the copper industry for the military coup of Chile's General Pinochet against President Allende. President Allende had nationalized the copper mines following his election. In our view (and that of many others), these concerns about TNCs remain valid today, though we believe they can be managed through appropriate policy regimes.

Strategic management of FDI can maximize its net benefits for developing countries.

Notwithstanding the important problems discussed above, FDI *can* be beneficial to developing countries if properly managed by host governments. This involves the design of a package of incentives, rewards and controls. There are many factors to consider when designing policy towards FDI – namely, the particular mix of countries involved (as source countries and host countries), the type of industry and firm, and the regulatory and the tax regimes in which the investment is undertaken (see below).

FDI policy should be seen as an integral component of a country's national development strategy.

The developing countries that have benefited most significantly from FDI and other links with TNCs are those that have managed these investments in a manner that is consistent with a national development strategy. Within this parameter, there is a range of policies towards FDI and TNCs that have proven effective in promoting industrialization and other economic goals.

Japan, Korea and Taiwan built their industrial foundations on the basis of restrictive policies towards FDI.[8] These countries permitted FDI only in certain sectors, and (except in special cases) prohibited more than majority foreign ownership in key sectors. Policymakers in the three countries mandated 'local content' requirements (that specified, for example, the proportion of local inputs used in the production process) in subsidiaries of TNCs. These requirements were initially set at a low level and then were increased over time. The government also established limits on the royalties that could be paid on technology licences by local partners of TNCs.

The governments of Japan, Korea and Taiwan designed their policies towards FDI with several objectives in mind. Policy was designed to encourage FDI only in sectors where its benefits would outweigh its costs; to ensure that TNCs transferred the right types of technology at the right price; to maximize the technological spillovers from TNC activities to the local producers of their inputs; to prevent TNCs from repatriating too much of their earnings; to restrict the export activities of their local subsidiaries; and to maximize the incomes and exports generated by TNCs.

The generally restrictive policies towards FDI in Korea and Taiwan coexisted with very liberal policies in some sectors. For example, policymakers established free trade zones (FTZs) or export-processing zones (EPZs) during the 1950s and the 1960s when the countries suffered from foreign exchange shortages. Within these zones, TNCs in sectors such as garment and toy production and electronics assembly were permitted to hold up to 100 per cent ownership and were exempt from other regulations (e.g. labour law) on the condition that they export 100 per cent of their output. FTZs were seen by policymakers as a useful – if somewhat unpleasant – device to be exploited for specific purposes at the early stage of economic development. FTZs were gradually phased out when the foreign exchange shortages that they were initially designed to ameliorate lessened.[9] This strategy towards FTZs is rather different from the way that they are used in many countries today, which treats the attraction of FDI to FTZs as a goal in itself.

Singapore and Costa Rica have aggressively courted TNCs within the context of a clear, well-articulated plan as to the types of foreign firms that they wished to attract and the terms on which these firms could enter the country. The governments of these countries appreciate that their small size makes development of large, indigenous private-sector firms difficult. For this reason, they decided to create an alliance with TNCs and sought to foster FDI of high and improving quality. The governments then undertook critical investments in particular types of infrastructure and education in order to maximize the country's chance that it would be attractive to the types of foreign investors that were targeted in the national development plan. The Costa Rican government's investment in supportive infrastructure and education helped to convince the Intel corporation to locate a major microchip factory in the country.

The governments of Singapore and Costa Rica adopted a more liberal stance towards FDI compared to that employed by Taiwan and, especially, Korea. But in all four cases, FDI policy was deliberate, aggressive and informed by national development goals.

By contrast, during the last decade or so many developing countries radically opened their borders to TNCs with little benefit to their economies. This is because engagement with TNCs was not driven by a clear strategy for national development. The result of liberalization without vision is usually FDI of the 'wrong' types. Much of this FDI involves foreign investment in real estate development and takeovers of existing firms ('brownfield' FDI) with little injection of new technology. A lot of brownfield FDI has been tied to the privatization of state-owned enterprises motivated by fiscal reasons, rather than to a carefully conceived industrial strategy (see Chapter 8.1).

In the process of conflating a laissez-faire FDI policy with a national FDI strategy, many countries have granted foreign firms unnecessarily large subsidies (or tax exemptions, also known as tax holidays), abolished ownership restrictions for TNCs, reduced restrictions on profit repatriation, abolished local content requirements, liberalized regulations on technology transfer, and granted unnecessarily generous exemptions from national regulations (such as on labour and the environment). This phenomenon is often referred to as the 'race to the bottom'. The race to the bottom has had numerous negative effects on the tax base, living standards, and social and environmental conditions in developing countries.

In the long run, the lack of a coherent national industrial and FDI strategy means that countries are unlikely to upgrade their economies by wisely utilizing the investment resources and the foreign exchange generated by the FDI that they do attract. Note that the race to the bottom may be further intensified if a neoliberal multilateral investment agreement is adopted through the WTO (as a consequence of pressure by industrialized countries).

> Evidence shows that foreign investors do not shun countries that regulate FDI.

The race to the bottom is not only costly for developing countries. It is also not the most effective strategy for attracting FDI. Empirical studies find that the regulatory regime is not the most important determinant of foreign investment decisions. Far more important to the location decisions of foreign investors are factors such as economic growth, the size of the domestic market, the presence of sound infrastructure and a well-educated and disciplined labour force. Even the World Bank, an institution that is often associated with liberal policies towards TNCs, argues that '[t]he specific incentives and regulations governing direct investment have less effect on how much investment a country receives than has its general economic and political climate, and its financial and exchange rate policies' (World Bank 1985: 130).

China and Vietnam are examples of countries that are successful in attracting FDI despite the fact that they regulate it fairly aggressively. Foreign investors find these countries highly attractive because of their large domestic markets, rapid economic growth, and relatively well-educated labour force with what may be thought of as a good work ethic. The experiences of Singapore and Costa Rica, and more recently India, demonstrate the importance of a well-educated labour force in the attraction of FDI.

FDI policy should be designed on the basis of empirical evidence on the factors that influence location decisions. The evidence shows quite clearly that *TNCs enter – rather than create – economically dynamic countries*. In other words, growth leads to

FDI rather than the other way around as many neoliberals suggest (Milberg 1998).

Not all TNCs will exit countries that restrict their activities.

Policymakers in developing countries often overlook the fact that the risk of flight (especially over the short and medium term) does not apply equally to all types of TNCs. This is important because policymakers often assume that any attempt to regulate TNCs will cause them to exit the country. In fact, this fear is not warranted in many cases.

There exist only a relatively small number of industries where investments are highly mobile, and hence where investors can easily flee if the regulatory climate is no longer attractive to them.[10] Garments, shoes, textiles and stuffed toys are among the most mobile types of production. By contrast, investments in other industries are far less footloose. In many industries (such as chemicals and steel), production requires a significant initial investment in dedicated capital equipment. This means that relocation is very costly and time-consuming, and therefore would not be undertaken lightly. In other industries (such as advanced electronics and automobiles), relocation may be physically easier because the machinery and equipment of the production process may be more mobile. In practice, however, it is very difficult to relocate these firms because production depends on reliable subcontracting networks and other types of relationship that are not easy to establish elsewhere.

The bottom line is that not all investment by TNCs is equally subject to flight. The misplaced fear of flight should not discourage governments from regulating FDI as part of a national development strategy.

Policymakers should be aware that FDI sometimes causes substantial outflows of capital.

Following the numerous financial crises in developing countries during the 1990s, the apparent stability of FDI has led many people to treat FDI as the 'Mother Theresa of capital inflows', as the Cambridge University economist Gabriel Palma put it. However, it should be noted that FDI can cause substantial outflows of capital.

These outflows occur whenever the profits associated with foreign investment are taken out of the country where they are initially earned. TNCs are increasingly able to withdraw large pools of capital from host countries because many countries have eliminated restrictions on profit repatriation. Additionally, transfer pricing remains an important strategy for TNCs. Transfer pricing enables TNCs to repatriate pools of capital that exceed the profits they have actually earned in the host economy.

Additionally, in liberalized, internationally integrated capital markets, there is no limit on the ability of foreign (direct) investors to move vast sums of money out of the host economy by using their assets as collateral for loans drawn on domestic banks. These loan proceeds can then be converted into foreign currencies and invested abroad. Thus, like other forms of capital flows (such as PI), unregulated FDI has the potential to cause significant resource outflows from developing countries. Careful management of the terms of FDI can prevent or mitigate its potential to generate resource outflows.

Policy alternatives

Historical experience and empirical studies reveal two key lessons about FDI and involvement with TNCs.

First, there is no single template for managing FDI and other TNC activities. Governments in developing countries should maximize the potential for FDI to promote economic, and especially industrial, development by creating employment, increasing living standards and promoting the transfer of knowledge and technology.

As we have seen above, the historical and empirical record reveals that there are many different paths for achieving this aim.

The ability to manage FDI and other TNC activities depends on several factors, such as the host country's relative bargaining position (which itself may depend on country size), the technological nature of the industry, and the importance of the particular firm or industry in the government's overall national development vision.

Some countries in East Asia offer particularly good recent examples of strategies for maximizing the developmental benefits of FDI and other forms of TNC involvement. The recent experience of China, India and Vietnam demonstrate that foreign investors will not necessarily shun countries that place restrictions on their activities. These experiences show that management of FDI is still possible today. Evidence also shows that, when making investment decisions, TNCs place greater emphasis on factors like a large domestic market, an educated workforce, rising incomes and economic growth, and sound infrastructure rather than on a liberal regulatory regime.

Second, FDI policy stands the best chance of achieving developmental objectives if it is firmly tied to national development and/or industrial policy plans. Countries like Korea and Taiwan are known to have used strict regulation on FDI in most industries, while also taking a very liberal attitude towards FDI in others. This mixture of restrictive and liberal policies was possible because the governments developed a clear FDI strategy that differentiated among industries. The recent experiences of Singapore and Costa Rica show that policymakers can target the attraction of particular types of FDI (or even target particular firms) as a central part of their industrial or development strategy (see also Chapter 7.2).

> The precise strategy towards FDI should depend on the nature of the FDI that is being sought, the country's endowments, and the goals of the country's industrial policy regime.

Some countries, especially the poorest ones, may have rather narrow goals for FDI, seeking only an infusion of foreign capital that will increase employment (under any terms) and foreign exchange earnings. The garment industry, shoe production and toy manufacture often function in this limited but, in some cases, economically important capacity. In such cases, it may be acceptable – or even important – that the country maintain a relatively liberal attitude towards FDI because the industries are seen strictly as a 'cash cow'. Many countries have established EPZs for the purpose of attracting FDI to these types of industries. However, it should be noted that cash-cow industries tend to be 'dead ends' in the long run. Therefore policymakers need to devise a strategy to reinvest the export earnings generated by such industries in order to generate new industrial capabilities.

In some countries and in some industries, the government may find it necessary to induce foreign investors to undertake expensive investments in capital equipment and technology. These types of foreign investment can sometimes be a precondition for using the country's natural resources to some advantage because the technology necessary to extract natural (e.g. mineral) resources is not always available domestically. In this context it may be necessary to adopt an FDI strategy for this sector that is attractive to foreign investors, but that nevertheless allows the host country to extract the largest possible 'rent' from their own natural resources. Carefully structured joint-operating agreements have worked well in some countries.

In some cases, the government may seek to promote certain industries as part of an industrial policy plan aimed at creating long-run international competitiveness in some realm. At the early stages this might necessitate a major injection of new technology and capital, a circumstance that necessitates TNC participation. In this type of situation, it is important for the national government to negotiate with TNCs over technology transfer and to prevent TNCs from imposing restrictions on export and R&D. These matters were rather well negotiated in the cases of the Chinese auto industry and the Korean fast train project in the mid-1990s.

Finally, in those cases where the country is reasonably close to achieving international competitiveness in a particular industry, it may be necessary to exclude TNCs altogether. This is especially important where the domestic market is small. This restriction may be necessary so that local firms have the greatest possible opportunity to develop their competitive advantage.

The main point is that there is no single appropriate strategy for all types of FDI and TNCs and for all types of country. Each industry serves different functions in the greater scheme of industrial development. Policies towards FDI and TNCs must be tailored to the particular conditions of each industry and each country. FDI and TNC policy must be dynamic so that policy evolves as internal and external conditions change.

> Developing countries do have some bargaining power vis-à-vis TNCs, and this power should be exploited whenever possible.

It is, of course, one thing to say that countries should use TNCs in a strategic manner, and it is another to say that they can actually do so. Developing countries that are extremely poor, small or poorly endowed with natural resources hold far less bargaining power than countries with better 'initial conditions'. This is especially the case because poorly endowed countries are often most attractive to precisely those industries where capital mobility is highest (such as garment production).

On the other hand, many developing countries do have some bargaining power, at least in relation to some industries. Some countries offer the prospect of a large and/or rapidly growing domestic market. Examples of such countries are China, India, Brazil and the rapidly growing East Asian countries. A large and/or rapidly growing market is particularly important in industries where transportation costs are relatively high and/or where proximity to the desired market is important.

Another element of bargaining power that is possessed by some countries is the presence of a well-educated, well-trained workforce (relative to its wage level). Notably, the formerly and presently Communist countries of Eastern Europe, Vietnam and China are best situated in this regard thanks, somewhat paradoxically, to their Communist legacies. Location is another advantage possessed by some developing countries.

Countries that have the locational (and legal) advantage of easy access to large markets with rich consumers are also well situated to negotiate with some foreign investors. The bargaining power of Mexico is increased by its proximity to the USA (and its NAFTA membership), and that of the Central European countries (such as the Czech and Slovak Republics, Poland and Hungary) is enhanced by their proximity to Western European countries and their forthcoming EU membership. The possession of rare, strategic or otherwise valuable mineral and other natural resources also enhances bargaining power.

Needless to say, a developing country will be in the best position to exercise its bargaining power if its economy is on a solid footing in the first place. In this connection, it is important to pursue appropriate economic policies in the many realms that are discussed throughout Part II of this book. It is also critical to have a government that is internally coherent and is politically and administratively capable of exercising its bargaining power vis-à-vis foreign investors and other actors.

Notes

1. Another category of international private capital flows is private remittances. Private remittances refer to international resource transfers between individuals. The most common type of remittance occurs when a family member who is working abroad sends funds (i.e. wage remittances) to a family member in the home country. The discussion that follows does not address remittances because neoliberals do not offer policy recommendations in this domain (and hence we do not offer alternatives to remittance policy). Note that for some smaller developing countries, such as in Central America and the Caribbean, remittances are the largest single source of foreign exchange. The World Bank (2003) reports that worker remittances now rank second

in importance only to FDI in overall external finance of developing countries as a whole.

2. However, strategically important developing countries, such as Turkey and Pakistan, received significant foreign aid from the USA following the events of 11 September 2001.

3. Note that the data presented are meant to be illustrative. The absence of consistent annual data on all international private capital flows frustrates efforts to calculate period averages.

4. The negative figure in 2002 means that payments to foreign lenders exceeded the amount of new loans extended to developing countries.

5. All data in this and the following paragraph are taken from World Bank (various years).

6. Note that the level, scope and method of paying the reserve requirement tax was, in fact, changed many times during the lifespan of the policy regime in both Chile and Colombia. See Grabel 2003a for details.

7. In contrast, the domestic currency will not be under pressure to appreciate significantly if FDI increases gradually.

8. Restrictions on FDI were not exclusive to the East Asian countries. Between the 1930s and 1993, Finland restricted foreign ownership in enterprises to 20 per cent. In the nineteenth century, the USA restricted FDI in industries like coastal shipping, mining and logging, while disadvantaging TNCs by banning the employment of foreign workers. See Chang and Green 2003 for additional details on the history of restrictions on FDI.

9. Note that in the mid-1980s, only 6 per cent of TNC subsidiaries in Korea (including those in the FTZs) were 100 per cent owned by the parent firm. This contrasts dramatically with the situation of Mexico and Brazil where 50 per cent and 60 per cent, respectively, of TNC subsidiaries were 100 per cent foreign owned (Evans 1987: 208).

10. Though recall that evidence suggests that regulation plays far less of a role in FDI decisions than is commonly thought.

Domestic Financial Regulation

The neoliberal view

> The state regulation of the financial system, or 'financial repression', that is popular in developing countries is counterproductive.

The archetypal financial system in developing countries is antithetical to economic development. The typical financial system is characterized by a heavy degree of state involvement and the domination by banks rather than by capital markets (i.e. stock and bond markets). This state of affairs is widely described as 'financial repression'.

Intense state involvement in the financial sector has a number of adverse consequences. The maintenance of low interest rates (particularly in the context of high inflation) encourages domestic savers to hold their funds abroad, and generally makes current consumption more attractive than saving in domestic financial institutions. Low savings rates also mean that domestic banks have an insufficient pool of savings from which to extend loans. State involvement in finance also leads to the fragmentation of domestic financial markets, with only a small segment of politically connected borrowers gaining access to low-cost credit. Disenfranchised borrowers must resort to unregulated, 'informal' (or 'curb') lenders who often charge exorbitant interest rates, or otherwise have to manage in the face of unmet needs for capital.

Financial liberalization is essential for growth and stability.

In view of the above problems, developing countries must liberalize their financial systems. A liberalized financial system based on competitive capital markets is central to the promotion of high levels of savings, investment, foreign capital inflows and economic growth. Domestic financial liberalization not only increases the level of investment, but also increases its efficiency by allocating funds across investment projects according to strict rate-of-return criteria and via arm's-length practices. Domestic financial liberalization eliminates inefficiency by eliminating the wasteful and corrupt practices that flourish under regimes of financial regulation, and it subjects borrowers and firm managers to the rigours of market discipline. The introduction of market discipline and the elimination of corruption improve the operating performance of financial institutions. The prospects for financial stability are consequently enhanced by sound financial sector performance.

Liberalization also encourages the creation of new instruments and markets in which to trade them. This process is termed financial innovation. Investment and financial stability are promoted by these new opportunities for risk diversification and dispersion. By increasing the availability of finance, liberalization also eliminates the need for informal (and often exploitative) financing arrangements, and allows borrowers to seek out those forms of investment finance that best meet the needs of their particular projects.

The finance provided through capital markets is widely regarded as preferable to other forms of finance because it has a greater ability to disperse risk, it is allocated according to objective efficiency and performance criteria, it is cheaper than other forms of external finance (such as bank loans), and it is highly liquid. This last attribute is especially desirable: it encourages sound business management by placing managers under the threat of investor exit (or higher capital costs) if they underperform. (See Chapters 8.1 and 9.3 for further discussion of the disciplining function of liquid forms of finance.) The promotion of internationally integrated capital markets has the added benefit of facilitating the rapid integration of developing countries into the global financial system.

> A sequenced approach to financial liberalization may be useful, but the ultimate goal should be a total financial liberalization.

As with the liberalization of international capital flows, some commentators argue that domestic financial liberalization should be sequenced. In this view, full domestic financial liberalization can be attained only once other sectors of the economy are well functioning and liberalized – that is, the liberalization of trade and other activities should precede financial liberalization. However, many other commentators reject arguments for sequencing because of the problems introduced by this strategy (see Chapter 9.1). Most importantly, whatever one's view is on the issue of sequencing, there can be no dispute that the ultimate goal should be total financial liberalization.

> Most developing countries have been successfully implementing domestic financial liberalization since the mid-1970s.

Chile, Argentina and Uruguay were among the first developing countries to liberalize their domestic financial systems in the 1970s. These programmes encountered problems by the early to mid-1980s, but this happened only because they were implemented in the broader context of incomplete and inconsistent programmes of economic reform. Policymakers in the developing world have learned from these experiences; since then, financial liberalization has been implemented with far fewer problems. Since the 1990s the pace of domestic financial liberalization has accelerated dramatically to the benefit of developing countries.

Rejection of the neoliberal view

> Domestic financial liberalization in developing countries has had few ambiguous successes and numerous unambiguous failures.

The drive towards domestic financial liberalization in developing countries is fuelled by several mutually reinforcing developments. These include the growing importance of international private capital flows to developing countries (see Chapter 9.1), the global shift towards neoliberal economic policy, and the increased influence of financial interest groups and the IMF on the decisions of national governments.

Domestic financial liberalization has registered few successes. Some large firms in developing countries, especially in the context of privatization programmes, have received significant finance through the capital markets created or expanded under financial liberalization. The finance provided to these firms has often been cheaper than that available via bank loans. Financial liberalization has furthered the integration of developing countries in global financial markets.

However, even these modest achievements are tainted. The growth of large firms has increased business concentration in developing countries. Capital markets reinforce rather than undermine an existing dualism with regard to access to lower-cost external finance by large firms. The lower-cost capital that is available to some large firms has often fuelled speculative excess. And global financial integration has a downside in so far as it increases systemic risk, financial fragility and volatility, and increases the potential for financial crisis in developing countries (see Chapter 9, and especially section 9.3).

A large body of empirical evidence finds that domestic financial liberalization has unambiguously failed to deliver most of the rewards claimed by its proponents (e.g. Arestis and Demetriades 1997; Williamson and Mahar 1998). Domestic savings have not responded positively to financial liberalization. Financial liberalization has not promoted long-term investment in the type of projects or sectors that are central to economic development and to the amelioration of social ills (such as unemployment). Financial liberalization has created the climate, opportunity and incentives for investment in speculative activities and a focus on short-term financial as opposed to long-term developmental returns. The creation of a speculative bubble may temporarily result in an increase in investment and economic activity. But an unsustainable and financially fragile environment, or what Grabel (1995) terms 'speculation-led development', is hardly in the long-term economic interest of developing countries.

> Financial liberalization usually leads to 'speculation-led development', which in turn almost invariably ends in currency and banking crises. It also increases income inequality, creates disparities in political and economic power, and increases financial fragility.

Speculation-led development is highly problematic for several reasons. Contrary to the neoliberal view, the financial innovation and associated increase in liquidity that follow liberalization impart greater risk and instability to the financial system and the economy. The promotion of capital markets (especially when they are internationally integrated) exacerbates the problem of financial fragility. These risks frequently culminate in national financial crises, the burdens of which fall disproportionately on economically vulnerable and politically weak groups within society.

Indeed, many empirical studies find that financial liberalization often leads to currency and banking crises in developing countries (see Grabel 2003b, and references therein). Chile, Argentina and Uruguay experienced financial collapses following their experiment with financial liberalization in the 1970s. Since then we have seen financial crises follow liberalization in a great many developing countries, such as Russia, Nigeria, Jamaica, Korea, Thailand, Indonesia and Mexico.

Speculation-led development also aggravates existing social ills by increasing income inequality. This is because only a small proportion of the population is situated to exploit the opportunities for speculative gain that are available in the liberalized financial environment. Speculation-led development creates a small class of financiers who maintain greater economic ties to financial markets abroad than to those in their own country. In this context, political and economic power is shifted to the domestic and international financial community.

In a speculation-led economy the financial community becomes the anointed arbiter of the 'national interest'. This means that policies that advance the economic interests of the financial community (such as those that promote low inflation, high interest rates, low levels of public expenditure) are justified on the basis that they serve the broader public interest when this is simply not the case (see Chapter 11.2–11.3).

> A market-based allocation of capital is not the best means for promoting investment that is socially necessary. Nor is it a magic cure for inefficiency, waste and corruption.

Proponents of financial liberalization emphasize the benefits of market allocation over state allocation of capital. There is, however, no demonstrated empirical or historical relationship between a market-based allocation of capital and economic development. This is not surprising since the allocation of capital in market-based systems relies on private financial returns (i.e. profits) as the singular yardstick of investment success. And the private financial return on an investment can be quite different from its developmental or social return. For example, the developmental return on an investment in the provision of clean drinking water is likely to exceed its private return. The divergence between private and developmental returns means that alternatives to the market-based allocation of capital are necessary to promote investment that is socially necessary, but not necessarily privately profitable.

Financial systems that are characterized by corrupt or inefficient practices under regimes of financial control maintain these attributes even after liberalization. Liberalization frequently changes the form, but not the level, of corruption or inefficiency. The situation of Russia after financial liberalization exemplifies this point, but the country is by no means exceptional in this regard. As the US corporate scandals in 2002–03 demonstrate, corruption and inefficiency can occur on a rather large scale even in a highly liberalized financial system.

> Liberalized financial systems have not been a part of most development successes.

The world's most successful development experiences occurred in countries where the state effectively managed the financial sector so that it served the goals of economic development, or where the financial and industrial sectors functioned as partners in the development process (often, although not always, under the guidance of the state).

The landmark historical study of economic development conducted by the economic historian Alexander Gerschenkron (1962) found that state institutions and financial–industrial ties were critical to the success of the world's late industrializers. He found that state institutions and linkages between finance and industry were more important the later a country started industrialization. Gerschenkron's study of the development experiences of Continental European countries, Japan, Russia and the USA demonstrated that there was no single template for successful economic and financial development. This is hardly surprising since these countries have diverse institutional, political, cultural and economic capacities. Nevertheless, his historical findings do illuminate the fact that liberalized financial systems and arm's-length financial arrangements have been part of the development experience of very few of today's industrialized countries. The same is true of the high growth eras in most developing countries.

It is worth noting that the financial systems of the USA and England were more liberal than those of their peers during industrialization. Early US economic development was, however, characterized by dramatic speculative bubbles, low levels of confidence in the financial system, and recurrent, serious financial crises. Until the early twentieth century, the practice of insider trading and various types of financial corruption were also rampant in the USA. The country only overcame its chronic financial instability in the mid-twentieth century through the creation of a sound financial infrastructure involving numerous regulatory bodies and a central bank, well-funded systems of deposit and financial insurance, a sound banking system, the enforcement of disclosure laws, and a high level of technical capacity by financial actors (Chang 2002: ch. 3).

English financial development, while less chaotic than that of the USA, was not as market-oriented as is generally thought. The monetary policies of the Bank of England were directed by the government, and were significantly influenced by the country's powerful financial community. The Bank of England frequently mitigated the country's financial difficulties by working closely with the central banks of other powerful, wealthy countries (especially France). And the English financial and economic system benefited greatly from the significant direct and indirect resource transfers associated with colonialism. England's status as the first country to industrialize on a large scale also meant that the challenges of competing in the global economy were irrelevant until other countries started challenging, ultimately successfully, its economic supremacy.

> The financial systems of the USA and Britain have been highly liberalized since the mid-1980s. Many studies of these systems conclude that liberalization has served the needs of all but the financial sectors in these countries very poorly.

Studies have found that the liberalized financial environment in Britain and, especially, in the USA has forced firm managers to focus excessively on short-term performance and stock market valuation (see Grabel 1997, and references therein). In this climate, firms are penalized (through the decline in their stock price) for undertaking investments that bear fruit only over the long term, such as R&D. They are also rewarded for decisions that reduce costs, such as firing employees or relocating to countries where wage costs are lower.

The takeover mechanism associated with the stock markets of the USA and Britain has not benefited their economies (see Chapter 8.1). The threat and the actuality of takeovers have aggravated the 'short-termism' of corporate managers, have resulted in a greater degree of concentration and monopolization of business, and have induced job losses in many sectors.

Evidence from the USA suggests that the large banks that generally flourish in liberalized financial environments are not conducive to the growth of small and medium-size businesses (Berger et al. 2001). A study of large banks in the USA finds that they are less willing to lend to small firms than are smaller banks. This finding should give policymakers in developing countries an additional reason to be cautious on the matter of abandoning restrictions on cross-border and domestic bank mergers as this can aggravate the serious financing constraints already faced by small firms within their economies.

In sum, the myriad problems associated with financial liberalization and takeovers are hardly worth exporting to developing countries.

Policy alternatives

> The goal for domestic financial regulation: finance in the service of development. The principal criterion for evaluating the performance of the financial system: functional efficiency.

Domestic financial regulation in developing countries should be guided by one fundamental consideration: the financial system should operate in the service of sustainable, stable and equitable economic development. The chief function of the financial sector in developing countries is to provide finance in adequate quantities and at appropriate prices for those investment projects that are central to this kind of development. All financial reforms should be evaluated against the extent to which they achieve this aim. Domestic financial reforms that improve the functioning of the financial system along other dimensions (such as liquidity, international integration, etc.) should be seen as secondary to the primary developmental goal of the financial system.

We submit that the most important way in which the financial system can serve appropriate economic development is through the provision of long-term finance, which is necessary to the viability of most projects that are central to economic development (e.g. investment in infrastructure and the promotion of infant industries). In his research on the US financial system, economist James Tobin (1984) uses the term 'functional efficiency' to refer to the ability of the financial system to provide finance for long-term investment. The concept of functional efficiency contrasts with the more conventional notion of efficiency that focuses on the pricing mechanism – for example, whether the cost of a bank loan accurately reflects the private risk associated with a particular investment. Any proposed financial reform should be evaluated based on its ability to contribute to functional efficiency.

Strategies for creating financial systems that serve the goals of development.

The goal and performance criteria advanced above can be operationalized in any number of ways. Needless to say, the appropriateness of the exact policy instrument(s) chosen depends on the particular conditions in each country, such as the character of the financial architecture, institutional capacities, and historical, political and economic conditions. However, there are some well-known mechanisms that many governments have used in order to influence, direct or coordinate the allocation of a significant proportion of financial flows.

Government influence over the price and direction of bank lending to key sectors was central to industrial development in Japan, most Continental European and East and Southeast Asian countries, and Brazil. Government influence over loan allocation may also involve the establishment of lending targets at the sectoral level that are imposed on private, quasi-private or publicly controlled banks. Alternatively, the government can use the tax system to influence bank lending. Tax incentives can encourage banks to lend to strategic firms or sectors. A system of lending targets or tax credits can ensure that bank lending supports a range of identified social and economic goals.

Specialized lending institutions can also be established to serve particular mandates. These might include encouraging female and/or minority entrepreneurship, supporting the development of small and medium-size businesses, or promoting the development of new technologies (such as those that promote good environmental outcomes).

Another means of ensuring the provision of stable, long-term finance to particular sectors/firms is through the creation of development banks, which specialize in long-term financing. Development banks can be publicly financed and managed as in Brazil, Korea, Japan and France, or can be privately financed as in the case of German industrial banks. It is also conceivable that these banks could be organized as a public–private hybrid, and could raise capital on international markets and even from private donors. Development banks are the institutional counterpart of the industrial policies and public investment programmes that are critical to late development, as the experiences of several countries suggest (see Chapters 7.2 and 11.3).

Evidence from late developers shows that development banks and other specialized banks can be managed and regulated effectively. *The challenges of effectively managing these institutions are neither greater nor lesser than those associated with managing private banks in a liberalized environment.* Moreover, as Singh and Weisse (1998) argue, the resources used to create a liberalized financial system would be better spent in ensuring the appropriate and sound operation of a financial system that operates in the service of development.

Another means to ensure that the domestic financial system serves developmental objectives is a system of variable asset-based reserve requirements for financial firms. Palley (2000) advances a case for asset-based reserve requirements, and we augment this proposal modestly in the interests of exploiting its developmental potential. A system of variable asset-based reserve requirements has three chief components. First, all financial firms in the economy are required to hold differential reserves against different types of assets in their portfolio, such as stocks, bonds, mortgage, consumer or small business loans. Second, financial regulators establish and manipulate the required reserve ratio against each type of asset based on the government's objectives vis-à-vis encouraging certain types of investments and their evaluation of a number of factors, such as the risk associated with that asset and market conditions. Third, required reserves are held in non-interest-bearing deposit accounts at the central bank.

Variable asset-based reserves provide regulators with a means to encourage/discourage financial institutions to hold certain types of assets by reducing/increasing the ratio of required reserves that must be held against them, and thereby lowering/raising the cost of holding certain assets. Variable asset-based reserves provide regulators with both a means to target sectoral imbalances involving overinvestment in some sectors and underinvestment in others, and a means to use the financial system in the service of industrial policy goals (see Chapter 7.2). A system of variable asset-based reserves can also reduce the risk of financial crisis through two channels. Regulators can use the asset-based reserve requirements to deflate bubbles in particular asset markets as they emerge and before they culminate in financial crisis. The system also functions as an automatic stabilizer because it requires financial institutions to deposit additional reserve holdings whenever asset values rise or whenever new types of assets are created.

Whither domestic financial liberalization?

Policymakers may wish to embark eventually on a limited pro-gramme of domestic financial liberalization, particularly once the country's initial industrialization and growth objectives are attained. In this connection, two considerations merit mention.

First, the success of liberalized financial markets depends on numerous prerequisites, many of which are not met in developing countries and cannot be exported easily or quickly. The financial history of industrialized countries shows that a sound financial and regulatory infrastructure is essential to the successful operation of a liberalized financial system, and this infrastructure cannot be created overnight. Neoliberal reformers pay lip service to the concept of good governance, but then rush to install liberalized financial systems in developing countries that lack the requisite institutional and regulatory capacities to ensure that they are viable. The numerous financial crises in developing countries (in addition to US experience in the nineteenth and early twentieth centuries) illustrate the costs of this strategy.

Second, policymakers should adopt a conservative stance on liberalization. That is, liberalize only when the benefits are unambiguous and cannot be reasonably achieved through any other means. Any benefits associated with financial liberalization must be carefully weighed against its costs (namely, increased levels of systemic risk, volatility and short-termism, all of which increase financial fragility, and thus the chance of financial crisis). For example, liberalized capital markets have provided a greater volume of finance to 'start-up' enterprises than have more regulated systems. But this does not mean that financial liberalization is the only way to ensure the provision of finance to these enterprises or to other underserved sectors of the economy. Public investment, lending targets, tax credits, specialized lending institutions and variable asset-based reserves are other means for ensuring the provision of adequate finance to underserved sectors.

> Particular caution is warranted in two areas: the promotion of capital markets and off-balance-sheet activities.

If policymakers value financial stability, it is particularly important that they adopt restrictions on the introduction of liquid, internationally integrated capital markets and on the pace of financial innovation, especially when it involves creation of off-balance-sheet activities, such as derivatives. (See above on financial innovation and Chapter 9.3 on off-balance-sheet activities.)

As we have seen, liquid, internationally integrated capital markets carry few ambiguous benefits and myriad unambiguous costs, especially (but not exclusively) for developing countries. The case for promoting them is thus rather dubious. *If* capital markets are to be promoted at all, significant resources must be committed to minimizing their risks, narrowing the scope of their operation, and in ensuring that other segments of the financial system (such as banking) serve developmental objectives.

Off-balance-sheet activities (such as derivatives) are even more problematic, given their complete lack of transparency and the high degree of risk introduced by them. As we argue in Chapter 9.3, these activities have no place in developing countries.

11 **Policy Alternatives 5**

Macroeconomic Policies and Institutions

11.1 **Exchange Rate and Currency Policies**

Terminology

A convertible currency is a currency that holders may freely exchange for any other currency regardless of the purpose of conversion or the identity of the holder. In practice, this means that the central bank pledges to buy or sell unlimited amounts of the domestic currency (and if the exchange rate is set by the government, this commitment extends to guaranteeing the exchange at a predetermined price).

For example, say you found yourself holding the Mexican currency, the peso, but you did not wish to purchase any Mexican goods with your pesos. This is not a problem as the peso is fully convertible. This means you could purchase any other currency with your pesos. But if you were holding a non-convertible currency, such as the Chinese yuan, you might not be able to undertake this transaction. The transaction could only be undertaken if it were for certain pre-approved types of activity, following purchase of a foreign exchange licence (that entitles the holder to exchange currency), or following approval by the central bank or other monetary authority.

A floating exchange rate system is one in which the value of the domestic currency is determined by market forces. Under a system of floating exchange rates, an increase in demand for a country's currency (other things being constant) causes the currency to appreciate. Demand for a country's currency will increase, for example, whenever foreign investors purchase assets in the country (because they must obtain the currency before purchasing them). A decrease in the demand for a country's currency (other things being constant) causes the currency to depreciate. The demand for a currency will decrease whenever investors sell assets denominated in the currency, and then sell their holdings of the currency.

Floating exchange rate systems contrast with fixed or pegged systems in which the value of the currency is set by the government (fixed rates), or is allowed to fluctuate only within a narrow band (pegged exchange rates). The term 'crawling peg' refers to exchange rate regimes wherein the band in which the currency is permitted to fluctuate is adjusted based on changes in certain economic conditions, such as changes in the rate of inflation.

Some basic empirical facts

Today, most developing countries have convertible currencies and floating exchange rates. Most countries that are members of the IMF today maintain convertible currencies. Recent reports indicate that 151 countries (of the 183 that are IMF members) maintain fully convertible currencies. Recent studies report that about 60 per cent of all developing countries maintain some type of floating exchange rate regime (Bird and Ramkishen 2001).[1]

The neoliberal view of currency convertibility

> Currency convertibility is essential to the promotion of international trade and private capital flows.

Currency convertibility is essential for developing countries because foreign investors will be less willing to commit funds to a country if they face restrictions on their ability to convert any currencies earned through international trade and investment. Restricting currency convertibility gives rise to waste and corruption since individuals and firms will devote resources to evading convertibility restrictions (for example, by bribing the authorities to issue illegal foreign exchange licences).

The neoliberal view of exchange rate regimes

> Floating exchange rate systems are the ideal to which all developing countries should strive.

Floating rate systems are optimal because they give maximum play to market forces and thereby promote economic efficiency and discipline. In floating rate systems, the value of a country's currency provides important information about the economy. A country with an appreciating currency is one that has gained the confidence of investors (as evidenced by their purchase of domestic assets). A country with a depreciating currency is one that investors hold in lower regard.

Floating exchange rates also eliminate the potential for speculators to 'bet' that the government will be forced to change the rate or the range at which the currency is pegged. This type of speculation has often caused governments to devalue dramatically the rate at which their currency is pegged. In some cases, pegged exchange rate regimes have even collapsed under the weight of intense speculation against the currency.

Floating exchange rates promote a greater degree of financial stability than do fixed or pegged exchange rates. This is because there is no reason for speculators to test the government's commitment to maintaining a particular currency value.

> In some cases, extreme fixed exchange rate systems, such as currency boards, and even currency substitution are second-best alternatives to floating rates.

Floating exchange rates are not always feasible. This may be the case if the economy is too fragile to withstand the currency fluctuations associated with floating rates, if domestic and foreign investors place a high value on currency stability and predictability because of previous experience with currency crises or high inflation, or if monetary authorities cannot be trusted to abstain from intervening in the currency market. In those circumstances where floating exchange rates are not viable, extremely rigid fixed exchange rate regimes such as a currency board or even full currency substitution may be necessary.

The currency board is a politically insulated institution charged with guaranteeing that the domestic currency is fully convertible upon demand and without limit into a foreign reserve currency at a fixed rate of exchange. The fixed exchange rate is guaranteed by holdings of the reserve currency, generally a strong foreign currency such as the US dollar or the euro. The currency board can only issue additional domestic currency if holdings of the reserve currency are increased via export sales or foreign investment inflows to the country.

Full currency substitution involves legally replacing the domestic currency with a strong foreign currency. This strategy is sometimes referred to as dollarization, since the US dollar is the currency most commonly employed in full currency substitution arrangements.

In other words, only 'extreme' exchange rate systems (termed 'corner solutions' in the academic literature) are workable. On one end of the exchange rate continuum is the ideal of floating rates; on the other end are second-best systems of extreme exchange rate fixity embodied in currency boards or currency substitution. Exchange rate regimes that fall between the extremes of floating and extreme fixity (termed 'intermediate regimes' – fairly wide currency pegs or crawling-peg regimes) are destined to fail.[2]

> Some countries need the discipline and credibility associated with currency boards.

Currency boards have several desirable features. They maintain exchange rate stability and thereby prevent currency crises. They prevent high inflation by setting strict conditions on the circumstances under which the domestic money supply can be increased. And, finally, currency boards promote foreign investment and confidence by resolving problems of currency and price volatility and by delegating policy to an institution that divests corrupt or inept politicians from any influence over the national currency (see also Chapter 6 and section 11.2 below for similar arguments on behalf of independent central banks).

Today, currency boards operate in Bermuda, Bulgaria, Bosnia and Herzegovina, Cayman Islands, Djibouti, Estonia, Falkland Islands, Faroe Islands, Gibraltar, Hong Kong and Lithuania.

> For some countries, even currency boards do not offer sufficient discipline and credibility. In these cases, full currency substitution is necessary.

Full currency substitution is preferable to a currency board whenever the government cannot be trusted to respect the operational independence of the currency board or whenever policymakers seek the most rapid route to exchange rate stability and international credibility. As of 2001, twenty-three countries maintain full currency substitution, while fourteen countries maintain partial currency substitution. Countries that maintain full currency substitution include Ecuador, El Salvador, Panama, Northern Cyprus, and the British Virgin Islands; countries that maintain partial currency substitution include Cambodia, Liberia, Guatemala, Namibia and Tajikistan. Partial substitution refers to circumstances wherein the national currency circulates alongside a much more widely utilized foreign currency.

Rejection of the neoliberal view on currency convertibility

> Unrestricted currency convertibility creates the potential for currency depreciation and collapse, capital flight and financial instability. Conversely, restricting convertibility curtails these problems.

Maintenance of unrestricted currency convertibility is highly problematic from the perspective of financial stability (see Grabel 2003a). Investors cannot move their money freely between countries unless they can easily convert capital from one currency into another. But the practice of currency conversion and the sudden exit from assets denominated in the domestic currency expose the currencies of developing countries to pressure to depreciate. And as we have seen in Chapter 9 (especially section 9.3), large, sudden currency depreciations can initiate a vicious cycle of additional depreciation, a decline in asset values, and financial crisis.

Conversely, currencies that are not convertible cannot be placed under sudden pressure to depreciate because there are substantial obstacles to investors acquiring the currency in the first place. Moreover, to the extent that investors are able to acquire the currency (or assets denominated in it), their ability to liquidate these holdings is ultimately restricted. Thus the likelihood of a currency collapse (triggered by the sudden, large-scale exit of investors) is trivial because the currency cannot be attacked. The greater the restrictions on convertibility, the smaller is the scope for dramatic depreciation of the currency caused by sudden investor exit (and ultimately the smaller is the scope for currency collapse). Of course, it also follows that the greater the restrictions on convertibility, the greater are any costs associated with maintenance of these restrictions. Such costs may include the creation of a black market in the currency or bribery aimed at securing a foreign exchange licence. However, these costs (to the extent that they occur at all) are insignificant when compared to the benefits to financial stability associated with restricted currency convertibility.

Restricting currency convertibility can also curtail capital flight. Restricting convertibility can effectively discourage foreign investors from even buying the kinds of domestic assets that are most prone to flight (such as portfolio investment) because these holdings cannot be readily converted to their own national currency. To the extent that these restrictions do not discourage foreign investors from purchasing assets subject to flight in the first place, they nevertheless undermine their ability to liquidate these investments and take their proceeds out of the country. Convertibility restrictions also reduce the ability of nationals to move their wealth abroad because their ability to convert their own currency into other currencies is restricted. Hence, restricting currency convertibility reduces the possibility that the economy will be destabilized by a vicious cycle of currency depreciation and capital flight by domestic and foreign investors.

Note that restricted convertibility gives governments the opportunity to allocate scarce foreign exchange to priority sectors (consistent with industrial policy programmes; see Chapter 7.2).

> Most of the world's industrialized countries did not maintain unrestricted currency convertibility until their economies were strong and stable, and therefore could withstand the pressures of currency volatility.

The trend towards the adoption of unrestricted currency convertibility by developing countries today is in sharp contrast with that of the immediate post-World War II period when currency convertibility was rare. At that time, only the USA and four countries within its sphere of influence (namely, El Salvador, Guatemala, Mexico and Panama) maintained unrestricted currency convertibility. Indeed, countries in Western Europe and Japan did not even adopt limited convertibility until 1959 and 1964, respectively. The decision to move slowly towards unrestricted currency convertibility was motivated by the fear that these war-weakened economies could not withstand the pressures on their currencies brought about by capital flight.

In contrast, developing countries have been pressed to adopt unrestricted currency convertibility much earlier in their development than did Western Europe and Japan. This change in currency policy reflects the combined dominance of neoliberalism and the ability of the financial community and the IMF to influence policy in developing countries.

> Restrictions on currency convertibility today play an important role in promoting financial stability in economically successful countries such as China, India and Taiwan.

Some developing countries today maintain restrictions on currency convertibility. Some of these countries – namely, China, India and Taiwan – are quite attractive to foreign investors, have performed impressively with regard to international trade, and, most importantly, were largely unaffected by the Mexican and the Asian financial crises of 1995 and 1997, respectively. Restrictions on currency convertibility (coupled with other financial controls) protected these countries from the possibility of currency collapse and minimized the opportunities for capital flight. Investors in China, India and Taiwan did not panic during the Mexican and Asian financial crises because they had little reason to fear a collapse of currency and/or asset values precisely because of the limited convertibility.

In the case of China, for example, the currency is not convertible for a particular class of transactions, namely those that relate to the purchase or sale of domestic assets by foreigners in the form of FDI or PI. In the language of balance-of-payments accounting, this means the currency is not convertible for capital account transactions. Capital account transactions are singled out because they can introduce particularly high levels of financial risk to the economy (and thereby can render the economy vulnerable to financial crisis). The Chinese currency is convertible for transactions that relate to international trade in goods, however, and for those that relate to the repatriation of the profits that derive from foreign investments once they are undertaken. This is known as current account convertibility.[3] Restrictions on currency convertibility protected China from many of the difficulties that led to the collapse of so many economies during the Asian crisis. In fact, Chinese authorities intensified their enforcement of convertibility and other capital controls as the Asian crisis unfolded.

Restrictions on the convertibility of the Chinese currency mean that savers cannot legally use domestic currency holdings to purchase financial assets denominated in foreign currencies (e.g. US Treasury bills or Japanese company shares). The convertibility restrictions also prevent foreign and Chinese speculators from acting on a suspicion that the currency is overvalued and is therefore likely to fall. Foreign exchange can only be obtained if a buyer can demonstrate a need related to trade, tourism, repayment of approved foreign-currency loans, or the repatriation of profits derived from FDI. Similarly, access to 'futures markets'[4] for foreign exchange is limited to those with a documented need related to international trade. The Chinese government also tightly controls foreigners' access to the currency through licensing and permit requirements.

The Indian currency is also convertible for current account transactions only.[5] Offshore rupee transactions and dollar-denominated transactions between residents are prohibited. The access of individuals and firms to foreign currency (especially for what are deemed non-essential purposes) is strictly managed by the central bank. Authorities in Taiwan control access to foreign currency and restrict the use of derivative products denominated in the domestic currency. Restrictions on currency convertibility and/or currency access in India and Taiwan are motivated by the same concern for stability that drives currency policy in China.

Restrictions on currency convertibility *alone* did not protect China, India and Taiwan from the Asian crisis. But these restrictions did curtail the risks (and investor perceptions thereof) to which these economies were exposed (see also the discussion of complementary capital and financial controls in Chapters 9 and 10). It is noteworthy that a recent study of convertibility and capital controls by some IMF staff concludes that restrictions on convertibility and other financial controls in China and India can be credited with the performance of these economies during the Asian financial crisis (Ariyoshi et al. 2000). The report further notes that the stability benefits of the financial controls obtained despite some evasion and some reduction in efficiency.

Other developing countries, such as South Korea, restricted

currency convertibility until they embarked on financial liberalization beginning in the late 1980s. Restricted currency convertibility (along with a managed exchange rate and other financial controls) contributed to South Korea's strong economic performance and financial stability during its rapid growth era.

Neoliberals generally focus on the high costs of convertibility restrictions. For example, they often argue that convertibility restrictions may give rise to black markets, corruption and/or misinvoicing of trade transactions. But they overlook the fact that the resources devoted to these wasteful activities are dwarfed by the resources wasted in the currency speculation that frequently occurs in liberal financial environments. Moreover, the economic and social costs of financial instability and crisis tend to be much greater than the economic costs of convertibility restrictions.

Rejection of the neoliberal view of exchange rate regimes

The sudden, large changes in currency values that often occur in floating exchange rate regimes impose serious costs on developing countries.

In our view, most developing countries can ill afford the currency (and general financial) instability introduced by floating exchange rates. With floating exchange rates, a large-scale, sudden investor exit from the currency will cause the currency to depreciate. A vicious cycle of currency depreciation and investor flight is all too common in developing countries that maintain floating exchange rates and fully convertible currencies (see also Chapter 9). In addition to problems of financial instability, significant currency depreciations increase the cost of servicing foreign debts, the majority of which are repayable in foreign currency. Currency depreciations also raise the cost of imported goods, some of which, like medicine and food, may be essential.

As we saw in Chapter 9, sudden, large capital inflows can be as problematic as large capital outflows in the context of floating exchange rate regimes. A deterioration in net export performance and job losses in the export sector can result from the currency appreciation caused by sudden, large capital inflows.

> Currency boards and currency substitution are far from second-best alternatives to floating exchange rates. Indeed, there are few circumstances under which these alternatives are desirable.

Neoliberals ignore the serious and unacceptable economic, political and social costs of currency boards and currency substitution (see Grabel 2003c). We consider these costs in turn.

First, currency boards tie the hands of monetary and fiscal policymakers by precluding discretionary changes in economic policy. Under currency board rules, policymakers cannot implement expansionary monetary and/or fiscal policies when the deteriorating national economic climate makes such actions necessary (e.g. when unemployment rises or economic activity slows). From the neoliberal perspective, this may be a good thing, as it means that corrupt or inept government officials cannot use expansionary policies to gain political support. From our perspective, however, it is both irresponsible and unwise to eliminate the possibility of redressing economic and social problems through discretionary economic policy (see the analogous discussion of independent central banks in section 11.2 below). Moreover, countries with currency boards 'import' the monetary policy of the country to which their currency is bound. It is difficult to imagine that the monetary policy of an industrialized country such as the USA is appropriate to economic conditions in a developing country. Moreover, the USA might pursue contractionary monetary policy at a time when a developing country needs expansionary policy, owing to divergent macroeconomic conditions in the two countries.

Second, currency board rules reinforce a contractionary, neoliberal bias in macroeconomic policy. The operating rules of currency boards stipulate that the domestic money supply can be increased only following an increase in foreign exchange holdings. An expansion of the domestic money supply is then predicated on a country's ability to sell goods or financial assets in international markets. Thus, under currency board rules, an increase in the money supply is tied to the success of efforts to increase exports, liberalize capital flows and enhance investor confidence. Currency board rules also promote reductions in government spending by mandating that new money can be printed only if it is backed by new holdings of the foreign reserve currency. Note that this restriction also supports privatization programmes since it prevents the central bank from providing aid to unprofitable SOEs.

Countries with currency boards frequently experience severe recessions, high unemployment and social misery. These outcomes stem in large part from the contractionary policy bias associated with currency boards. The strictures of the Argentinean currency board may have temporarily resolved the country's problems with high inflation, but this 'achievement' came at an unacceptably high economic and human cost. Argentina's four-year recession, social unrest and government collapse are in no small measure the product of the highly restrictive policies associated with the currency board and with the government's ultimately unsuccessful efforts to salvage it.

Third, currency board rules hold domestic trade performance hostage to the performance of the reserve currency. This is because the value of the domestic currency is tied to that of foreign reserve currency (or currencies). Argentina's trade performance was greatly compromised by the exceptional strength of the US dollar to which its currency was tied (until February 2002).

Fourth, all currency boards are afforded the highest degree of political insulation. In our view, the delegation of exchange rate management to a politically insulated institution seriously comprises democracy and political accountability (see also Chapter 6 and section 11.2). This is especially objectionable because exchange rate policies can and do have substantial distributive effects. Hence, institutions charged with exchange rate management must be accountable to elected government officials and, thereby, to the electorate.

Last but not least, currency boards do not live up to the most basic claim that proponents make on their behalf. That is, currency boards do not prevent speculation against the national currency. The recent experience of Argentina clearly demonstrates that currency boards do not protect developing countries from the financial and economic collapse that is associated with speculation against their currencies.

We conclude that currency boards are of no use to developing countries because they fail to prevent speculation against the domestic currency and exact severe economic and political costs.

Full currency substitution is even more problematic than currency boards.

Full currency substitution induces all of the economic, political and social problems associated with currency boards. Full currency substitution undermines the state's fiscal ability. Governments that adopt full currency substitution not only lose the ability to finance expenditure by printing money, but also assume the cost of obtaining the foreign currency that will replace the national currency. These costs are difficult to calculate, though some studies attempt to do so. For instance, Velde and Veracierto (2000) estimate that full dollarization by Argentina would cost the government $658 million or 0.2 per cent of GDP per year.

Currency substitution dispenses with even the pretence that policymakers in developing countries should be permitted to exercise any policy autonomy whatsoever. Currency substitution compromises a powerful symbol of national identity and independence through the elimination of a national currency. This latter attribute frankly renders currency substitution (and even currency boards) a strategy that bears far too close a resemblance to the colonialism of earlier eras.

> Managed exchange rate regimes have played an important role in the development process in many countries.

Managed exchange rate regimes are those in which the convertibility of the domestic currency is restricted to some degree. A pegged exchange rate is one type of managed exchange rate system. In pegged rate systems, central banks intervene in currency markets in order to keep the exchange rate within a predetermined, publicly stated range. It is critical to acknowledge that pegged exchange rates are only sustainable if they are accompanied by capital controls. This is because high volumes of international capital inflows or outflows make it difficult for authorities to maintain a currency peg within a predetermined range.

Neoliberals declared pegged rate regimes dead following their collapse in the Asian crisis countries. But they neglect to mention that pegged exchange rates functioned extremely well in South Korea, Malaysia and Indonesia *until* authorities began to abandon capital controls in the context of financial liberalization in the late 1980s and early 1990s. Currency pegs played an important role in the export-led growth and financial stability achieved by these countries during their period of rapid growth. During much of the 1990s, Chile maintained a crawling peg that was supported by stringent controls on capital inflows. As in several Asian countries, the currency peg supported a strategy of export-led growth and enhanced financial stability.

It is also important to recognize that policymakers in industrialized countries recognized the value of currency pegs (supported by capital controls) in the context of the economic challenges that followed World War II. It was not until 1976 that industrialized countries formally codified their decision to abandon the pegged exchange rates that they utilized following the end of the war. For almost thirty years after World War II, industrialized countries benefited from the currency stability created by pegged exchange rates (and stringent capital controls). And even after the breakdown of the post-World War II currency pegs, European countries created the European Monetary System, the centrepiece of which was a system of pegged exchange rates.

Policy alternatives with regard to currency convertibility

> There are a variety of ways that currency convertibility can be managed.

The recent experiences of China, India and Taiwan, coupled with the historical experience of most industrialized countries, illuminate the benefits of restricted convertibility. The problems associated with the premature adoption of full convertibility are underscored by the recent financial crises in a large number of developing countries.

Historical and contemporary experience demonstrates that there are a variety of means by which currency convertibility can be managed. The government can manage convertibility by requiring that those seeking access to the currency apply for a foreign exchange licence. This method allows authorities to influence the pace of currency exchanges and distinguish among transactions based on the degree of currency and financial risk associated with the transaction. The government can suspend or ease foreign exchange licensing as a type of speed bump whenever trip wires indicate the early emergence of vulnerabilities (see Chapter 9).

As we have seen, the government can also maintain selective currency convertibility, such that the currency is convertible for current account transactions only.[6] It is important to note that the IMF's Articles of Agreement (specifically Article 8) allow for this type of selective convertibility.

Finally, the government can curtail (but not eliminate) the possibility that non-residents will speculate against the domestic currency by controlling their access to it. This can be accomplished by preventing domestic banks from lending to non-residents and/ or by preventing non-residents from maintaining bank accounts in the country. The Malaysian government took precisely these steps in the aftermath of the Asian financial crisis. It restricted foreigners' access to the domestic currency via restrictions on bank lending and bank account maintenance and by declaring currency held outside the country inconvertible.

Policy alternatives with regard to exchange rate regimes

> Systems of adjustable exchange rate pegs can support export-led growth and financial stability provided that capital controls are also in place.

In some pegged exchange rate systems, the range within which the currency can fluctuate is informal and/or is unknown to the public. Consistent with our support for accountability and transparency, we suggest that currency pegs should be a matter of public knowledge. We also maintain that there are good economic reasons to create mechanisms whereby currency pegs can be modestly adjusted as economic circumstances warrant (e.g. as inflation rates change).

In his proposal for a system of adjustable pegged exchange rates, Grieve Smith (2002) argues that central banks should review currency pegs at frequent intervals (say, monthly) so that small adjustments in rates can be initiated through central bank intervention. He also argues that adjustments to exchange rate pegs should be automatic and expeditious. Frequent, modest and automatic adjustments can minimize the scope for destabilizing speculation against a currency peg. In the absence of this type of adjustment framework, speculative pressures can build because of uncertainty about the timing and extent of intervention in currency markets.

To summarize: support for adjustable pegged exchange rate regimes is provided by the historical achievements of pegged rates in developing and industrialized countries and by the demonstrated economic and social costs of currency volatility in developing countries.[7] As discussed above, the sustainability of any pegged exchange rate system depends on the presence of capital controls (see Chapter 9).

11.2 **Central Banking and Monetary Policy**

Terminology

Central banks are charged with carrying out a country's monetary policy. Monetary policy refers to government actions that influence the money supply and market interest rates. Central banks use a variety of tools to achieve these objectives, such as purchasing or selling government bonds on the open market, or changing the rate of interest that it charges the individual banks to which it lends. In so far as interest rates represent the cost of credit, monetary policy critically influences the level of investment and expenditure, and thereby affects the price level and the rate of economic growth.

The neoliberal view of central bank governance

> Central banks must be independent of the government so that they are insulated from the vicissitudes and pressures of electoral politics.

Only properly trained, appointed, non-partisan technocrats are uniquely suited to design and implement monetary policy that is in the national economic interest. This is because they do not have to pander to the electorate (or segments thereof) in order to retain their jobs. If the central bank is subject to political pressure, self-interested politicians or government appointees will implement irresponsibly expansionary (i.e. low interest rate) monetary policy to secure political support. The government can also instruct them to 'print money' (or increase the domestic money supply through other means) to finance new government expenditure (see also section 11.3 below) – this is known as 'monetization' of government deficits. The long-term performance of the economy ultimately pays the price for the political decision to pursue such policy.

The neoliberal view of monetary policy

Price stability should be the principal goal of monetary policy.

The long-run national economic interest is best served by anti-inflationary monetary policy. This is because anti-inflationary policy has the unique ability to promote savings, lending and investment. Banks will extend medium- and long-term loans only if they are confident that their returns will not be undermined by price increases over the lifetime of their loans. Foreign and domestic investment likewise depends on the expectation that inflation will not undermine returns over the lifetime of the investment project.

Additionally, domestic residents will maintain deposits in domestic banks only if they are confident that inflation will not erode the return on their savings and if they expect prices on consumer goods to remain stable. If domestic residents fear inflation, they will hold their savings outside the country (as long as capital controls do not prevent them from doing so) and will hoard goods in anticipation of future price increases.

> Policymakers in developing countries have rightly taken up the causes of central bank independence and inflation targeting since the 1990s.

For over a decade, policymakers have taken steps to increase the independence of existing central banks or create independent central banks where they did not exist previously (as in the former socialist countries). These reforms are driven both by the widespread acceptance of the case for central bank independence and by IMF structural adjustment programmes (SAPs) that often explicitly tie financial and technical assistance to central bank reform. For example, in negotiations with Brazil in February–March 1999, the IMF pressed for and received assurances from the government that it would strengthen the autonomy of the central bank. Increased central bank independence was also among the preconditions attached to the IMF's December 1997 bail-out of South Korea and the April 2001 bail-out of Turkey.

The likelihood that independent central banks will pursue anti-inflationary policy is enhanced by the adoption of constraints on their operating practices. For example, SAPs often include the stricture that central banks do not monetize government budget deficits – that is, do not print new money in order to finance budget deficits.

Another constraint on central bank operations that is becoming increasingly prevalent is the practice of inflation targeting. In inflation-targeting regimes, the central bank's primary objective is to manage monetary policy such that inflation does not rise above a predetermined, announced range (usually around 2–3 per cent) during a specified time period. At present, eleven developing countries (namely, Brazil, Chile, Colombia, the Czech Republic, Hungary, South Korea, Mexico, Peru, Poland, South Africa and Thailand) have adopted some form of inflation targeting. Other countries (such as the Philippines) are moving in this direction as well.

Rejection of the neoliberal view of central bank governance

> Independent central banks do not pursue 'neutral', non-partisan monetary policies that are in the broad national interest.

Contrary to the claims of neoliberals, independent central banks (like all policymaking institutions, regardless of their governance structure) operate in accordance with the interests of some groups, and against the interests of others (Grabel 2000). Independent central banks are structurally biased towards the interests of the financial community, an interest group for whom low inflation is of paramount importance. While there are other interest groups that are also harmed by inflation (e.g. those living on a fixed income, such as pensioners), the economic interests of the financial community are most directly and profoundly harmed by inflation. It is therefore unsurprising that the financial community

– a community that is mobile, politically powerful, and maintains strong international ties – is such a forceful advocate of central bank independence, an institutional form that maximizes the opportunity for monetary policy that is in its interests.

Note that the industrial community and export-oriented producers (and those employed in their enterprises) do not share with financiers an obsession with the prevention of inflation through restrictive monetary policy. Industrialists are often damaged by increases in borrowing costs that result from increases in interest rates. In addition, export-oriented producers are also often harmed by the appreciation of the domestic currency that results from an increase in interest rates (see Chapter 9.1 and section 11.1 above). Thus the distributional effects of the monetary policy pursued by independent central banks are far from neutral.

The neoliberal embrace of democracy, transparency and public accountability at the rhetorical level sits uncomfortably with the support for entrusting monetary policy to an institution that embodies none of these principles (see also the discussion of currency boards in section 11.1 above and Chapter 6). Independent central banks are incompatible with principles of democratic governance, particularly because monetary policy has such profound distributional and macroeconomic effects.

> Empirical evidence demonstrates that greater central bank independence fails to reduce inflation and improve macroeconomic performance in developing countries.

Given the importance that neoliberals place on the anti-inflationary performance of independent central banks, it is odd that a vast empirical literature on the subject does not offer unambiguous support for this claim. The findings of numerous empirical studies force the conclusion that there is no clear relation between central bank independence and anti-inflationary outcomes in the developing country context (Eijffinger and de Haan 1996). Moreover, empirical evidence shows that central bank independence is not associated with higher rates of economic growth or employment

(Eijffinger and de Haan 1996), financial stability (as excess credit growth and stock and real estate price inflation often occur in the presence of independent central banks), budget balance or a reduced tendency for the central bank to monetize fiscal deficits (Sikken and de Haan 1998).

Some analysts have argued that central bank independence is necessary to attract the foreign capital flows that are so important to developing economies at the present time (Maxfield 1997). But here, too, the empirical evidence is ambiguous. It is difficult for foreign investors to assess the actual operational independence of a central bank (as this so often differs from its legal independence). It is also the case that foreign investors were and are quite willing to invest in countries that do not have independent central banks (such as many countries in East Asia prior to their crises, Russia, China, etc.), provided growth prospects and/or speculative opportunities remain attractive (see also Chapter 9.4).

> Embedded, politically accountable central banks can and do play important developmental roles in numerous countries.

The historical record clearly shows that central banks that are in tune with the development and social welfare goals of a nation have played a critical role in the development experience of nearly all industrialized countries. We can refer to such central banks as 'embedded' in the societies where they exist. This is not surprising since, as we have seen, most successful development experiences were associated with the subordination of finance (through a variety of means) to the objectives of economic development (see Chapters 9.2–9.3 and 10, and section 11.1 above).

The central banks of Japan and most Continental European countries were key players in the industrialization process. In these cases, central banks directly channelled subsidized credit to strategic sectors of the economy as part of industrial policy programmes or coordinated the distribution and price of credit allocated by the banking system (see Chapters 7.2 and 10, respectively). Politically accountable central banks were the norm in Europe until the drive towards monetary integration in the 1990s gave neoliberals the advantage in shaping European monetary reform, especially through the creation of the politically insulated European Central Bank.

Embedded, politically accountable central banks were also the norm in most developing countries up until the 1990s. For example, policymakers in most successful East Asian countries tightly circumscribed the role of the central bank and treated it as an important partner in the government's growth plans, not as an aloof guardian of prices and currency values.

Rejection of the neoliberal view of monetary policy

The inflation obsession is misguided and leads to monetary policy that undermines economic growth.

The costs of hyper-vigilance against inflation are extremely high, and we believe unacceptable. The obsession with inflation leads to monetary policy that imposes significant costs on living standards and economic performance (with regard to industrial activity, employment and economic growth). Moreover, the economic benefits of this strategy are also unclear. Numerous empirical studies suggest that moderate levels of inflation (which, depending on the study, range from 10 to 40 per cent) have little or no cost in terms of economic growth. These studies find that the economic costs of inflation are introduced only at very high levels of inflation (by which is meant inflation rates above 40 per cent per year). It is notable that this conclusion is shared by Robert Barro (1996), a prominent neoliberal economist and 'inflation hawk'. He finds that moderate levels of inflation (which he defines as inflation of 10–20 per cent per year) have low costs to economic growth, while inflation rates under 10 per cent per year have no negative effects on growth.

The results of other empirical studies support these findings. For example, a recent World Bank study of the link between inflation and economic growth in 127 countries from 1960 to 1992 concludes that inflation rates below 20 per cent have no obvious empirical significance for long-run growth (Bruno 1995). The study further finds that average growth rates fall only slightly as inflation rates approach 20–25 per cent. The Bank study concludes that countries reap economic growth dividends when they move from inflation rates in the three-digit range to inflation rates of 20 per cent per annum.[8] Epstein (2001) finds that for semi-industrialized countries, moderate rates of inflation (which he defines as annual inflation under 20 per cent) have no clear effect on economic growth, investment, and inflows of FDI. Finally, Bruno and Easterly (1996) find that moderate inflation (which they define as annual inflation of 15–30 per cent) can be sustained for a long time without serious economic cost. The authors offer Colombia as an example of just such a country.

Our brief review of empirical evidence makes clear that hyper-vigilance against inflation in developing countries is unnecessary. A recent study of the USA provides some indication of the costs to economic growth of this hyper-vigilance. It estimates that increases in inflation in the USA from 3 per cent to 10 per cent would cost about 1.3 per cent of US GDP, whereas the lost output associated with reducing inflation from 10 per cent to 3 per cent would result in output costs of about 16 per cent of GDP (Walsh cited in Epstein 2001). It is also the case that many developing countries have registered impressive increases in economic growth *despite* significant inflation. For example, in the 1950s and 1960s Latin American countries maintained both double-digit inflation and strong economic growth. During this time, Brazil exemplified a high-growth, high-inflation country. Japan and Korea also grew rapidly in the 1960s and the 1970s with relatively high inflation – the inflation rate in these countries was around 20 per cent, which was higher than that of many Latin American countries.[9]

Policy alternatives with regard to central bank governance

> Politically embedded and accountable central banks should
> be participants in national economic goals as they have been
> in many countries.

The extent to which politically embedded and accountable central banks contribute to economic development depends very much on the technical capacity of the country's policymakers, the overall soundness of the government's national development strategy, and the ability of the country's policymakers to carry out that strategy and ensure that the financial system plays a cooperative role in the achievement of its economic goals.

Central banks should be neither less nor more accountable to the government than are other institutions that play important roles in influencing the country's economic and social welfare. Clear, transparent objectives for monetary policy (see below) should be established, and central banks should work with the government to achieve identified developmental objectives.

Policy alternatives with regard to monetary policy

> Politically embedded and accountable central banks
> should be charged with pursuit of monetary policy that
> promotes economic growth, employment and social-welfare
> objectives.

Taking a page from the neoliberal book, monetary policy should have targets. But instead of concentrating on inflation, monetary policy targets should comprise broader economic and social-welfare goals. In this connection, monetary policy targets can seek to promote economic growth, employment and equality. The prevention of high rates of inflation should be pursued only as far as is consistent with these broader goals.[10]

11.3 **Fiscal Policy**

Terminology

Fiscal policy refers to government actions regarding revenues and expenditures. Government revenues derive from taxes (e.g. income tax, sales tax, value-added tax and tariffs) and from other income sources such as profits from state-owned enterprises or government-owned assets like land or stocks. Government expenditures comprise current expenditures (e.g. salaries of government employees and social security payments) and capital expenditure (e.g. investments in roads and the purchase of computers.)

The neoliberal view of expenditure policy

> Governments in developing countries cannot afford to maintain high levels of expenditure.

Excessive government expenditure stems from the highly politicized nature of economic policy in developing countries. Government officials purchase political support and repay favours via expenditure programmes that target important groups. Excessive spending is a very serious matter (indeed, it is far more serious than tax deficiencies), as fiscal profligacy introduces and/or exacerbates several socio-economic problems.

First, government expenditure on social programmes may create perverse incentives. For example, the presence of unemployment benefits undermines the incentive to seek employment. Second, government expenditure is inherently wasteful and inefficient because spending decisions are not subject to market discipline and are frequently distorted by the corrupt practices of self-seeking officials. By contrast, private expenditure by individuals and firms is inherently efficient, or, at the least, far *less inefficient* than public expenditure. Third, excessive government expenditure induces or aggravates budget deficits.

Budget deficits create inflationary pressures that undermine investor confidence. Budget deficits induce inflation because they increase the level of demand in the economy and because the central bank often increases the money supply in order to monetize the budget deficit (see section 11.2 above). More importantly, the government borrowing that is necessitated by budget deficits discourages, or, in academic jargon, crowds out, private investment. Crowding-out occurs because the increased demand for loans by the government places upward pressure on the interest rate, which prices many private borrowers out of the market.

> Excessive expenditure is the problem; fiscal restraint is the solution.

In order to solve the expenditure problems of developing countries, policymakers must learn, or be compelled, to exercise fiscal restraint. It is therefore appropriate that radical expenditure reduction is a common component of the reforms mandated in exchange for IMF assistance. In certain cases, it may even be necessary to enforce prudence via externally enforced fiscal targets – necessary whenever investors have reason to be sceptical about a government's resolve. The Argentinian government implemented a widely publicized 'zero deficit law' (now unfortunately abandoned) in July 2001, which required the federal government to limit expenditure to available revenue. In exchange for this commitment, the IMF extended an $8 billion assistance package to the country in August 2001 (naturally withdrawn once it became clear that the government would not honour the obligations of the zero deficit law).

The neoliberal view of revenue policy

> The tax system in developing countries is plagued by problems of evasion. Developing countries also tend to rely heavily on distorting forms of taxation, such as tariffs.

Developing countries confront serious problems with the collection of corporate, income and property taxes at federal and local levels. For this reason, developing countries must rely on international trade taxes (namely, tariffs), taxes that are administratively more difficult to evade than are corporate and income taxes. Indeed, the importance of tariffs to overall tax revenue distinguishes developing from industrial countries: according to a recent study, the ratio of trade taxes to GDP in developing countries was 5.13 per cent compared to 0.72 per cent in industrialized countries.[11] Generally, the significance of trade taxes in overall tax revenue is inversely correlated with a country's wealth: for example, the African continent has the highest ratio of trade taxes to GDP among regions in the developing world.

However, raising tax revenue via trade rather than income or corporate taxes is highly problematic since trade taxes introduce all manner of distortions and inefficiencies to the economy (see Chapter 7.1 for discussion of tariffs).

Tax reform must focus on reducing evasion.

In view of the tax problems discussed above, developing countries must enhance tax collection.

The efficiency of tax collection and government expenditure may be enhanced by the creation of politically independent fiscal authorities (see, e.g., Mas 1995). (See sections 11.1 and 11.2 above, respectively, for parallel discussions of currency boards and independent central banks.) However, it must be noted that the success of independent fiscal boards depends on many factors, such as whether their independence will actually be maintained in practice, the competence of their staff, and funding of this new agency (World Bank 2002: ch. 5).[12] Tax collection may also be enhanced by the institution of a value-added tax (VAT), which is harder to evade than other types of tax. However, the success of a VAT, too, depends on the capacity of the agency that administers it.

Rejection of the neoliberal view of expenditure policy

The pattern of expenditure reductions promoted by neoliberals damages living standards and compromises immediate and long-term economic activity.[13]

Following every financial crisis, the IMF has pressed for expenditure reductions in a range of domains. Data show that the most common areas of fiscal retrenchment are social spending (encompassing health care and education) and spending on industrial and agricultural development, power, transport and communications. These reductions have had disastrous effects on social conditions and the living standards of the poor and middle class, and have induced serious recessions and jeopardized the economy's long-term performance. The fact that a significant proportion of total expenditure reduction falls upon those groups with the least political and economic power is rather unsurprising (though no less tragic). A crisis is precisely the time when government spending on social programmes and government support for industry, agriculture and infrastructure are most needed. Moreover, reductions in expenditure on industry, agriculture and infrastructure are particularly short-sighted since these expenditures are critical to long-term economic performance.

There is simply no evidence to sustain the view that spending by the private sector will replace government spending during a crisis – indeed, a retraction in spending by the private sector is a far likelier scenario. Indeed, even the IMF has had to recognize that the expenditure reductions (and the contractionary monetary policy) pressed upon Asian economies following the financial crisis of the late 1990s went too far. The post-crisis austerity in many Asian countries induced rather severe social dislocation, political instability, and a dramatic reduction in overall economic activity.

> The obsession with budget deficits obscures some of the real causes of imbalance – namely, the pursuit of certain aspects of the neoliberal agenda.

Neoliberals fail to recognize that some of the very policies that they promote exacerbate budget deficits. For example, trade liberalization diminishes tariff revenue, which is more important the poorer is the country (see above). Thus, it is a matter of simple arithmetic that fiscal imbalances will necessarily arise following trade liberalization, even though things like expenditures and other tax revenues are unchanged.

In some countries, privatization revenues have temporarily offset some of the tariff revenue lost due to trade liberalization. But the potential to offset lost tariff revenue in this manner is limited by the finite nature of potential privatization projects. To date, studies of privatization demonstrate that its potential to raise revenue and reduce budget deficits in the long run is limited.

Global neoliberal financial reform also plays a role in fiscal imbalances in developing countries. These reforms contribute both to the increase in interest rates on foreign loans and to the overborrowing by (and overlending to) business and governments in the developing world, as commercial banks replace governments and multilateral agencies as the primary lenders (see Chapters 9.2 and 10). Currency depreciations, which have become common in an era of flexible exchange rates, also increase the cost of servicing foreign debts (see section 11.1 above). The high cost of foreign debt service is a crucial factor in the growth of budget deficits in developing countries. Latin American countries are prime examples of countries that have large budget deficits that are significantly due to the cost of servicing their foreign loans.

It is ironic that neoliberal trade and financial reform – rather than the profligate spending that neoliberals associate with failed Keynesianism – contributes importantly to fiscal deficits. Indeed, a recent study finds that the combined effect of the higher interest payments on government debt associated with financial liberalization and the loss of tax revenue associated with trade liberalization can lead to a 6–7 per cent increase in the fiscal deficit (Toye 2000).

The IMF often requires that developing countries not only balance their budgets, but that they do so each year over the course of a structural adjustment programme. Even if one were to accept the inherent virtues of a balanced budget (which we do not), this annual requirement does not make sense. It would be far more reasonable to recommend that countries balance their budgets over a business cycle, so that government spending can be increased (reduced) in order to offset the reduction (increase) in private-sector spending during the recession (boom).

Fiscal policy should not be constrained by an obsession with budget balance.

The obsession with budget balance in developing countries is misguided. Budget deficits alone do not undermine investor confidence, cause inflation or discourage private investment. Empirical evidence shows that foreign and domestic investors do not shun countries with high deficits, provided that growth prospects are sound and/or attractive investment opportunities are available.

The neoliberal claim that budget deficits must always be avoided because they cause inflation is not supported by evidence. The increase in economic activity that is associated with government spending does not necessarily cause inflation in countries with significant excess capacity (as is the case in most developing countries). Empirical evidence does not support the claim that central banks generally monetize budget deficits by increasing the money supply (and thereby causing inflation). Careful study of this matter by Sikken and de Haan (1998) has demonstrated that the relationship between budget deficits and the money supply in developing countries is far more complex than most neoliberals acknowledge.

Historically, periods of rapid economic growth in Continental Europe, the USA and Japan were associated with large programmes of public expenditure and even large budget deficits.

The significant domestic public expenditure of the post-World War II era was complemented by the vast international public expenditure that was associated with the Marshall Plan. Industrialized countries engaged in very high levels of public expenditure during the rapid growth era of the 1960s. For example, in 1960 the ratio of public expenditure to GDP was 31 per cent in Sweden, 32.4 per cent in Germany, 27.2 per cent in the USA and 32.2 per cent in the UK (Navarro 2001). More recently, targeted public expenditure played a key role in the rapid growth of the Asian NICs. Public expenditure in Latin America in the 1940s to 1960s (particularly in Brazil, Argentina and Mexico) contributed to the region's impressive economic growth during this time. It is impossible to explain the growth experiences surveyed here without highlighting the role of government expenditure.

Even as neoliberals preach the virtues of fiscal restraint and balanced budgets, industrialized economies maintain high levels of public expenditure. A significant proportion of their public expenditure is deficit-financed. In 1999 the ratio of public expenditure to GDP was 55.1 per cent for Sweden, 44.8 per cent for Germany, 43.2 per cent for the Netherlands, 32.7 per cent for the USA and 37.8 per cent for the UK. High levels of public expenditure in industrialized countries are made possible by their impressive tax base and success in tax collection. It is therefore critical that policymakers in developing countries consider carefully the effects of any policy change on the tax base and that they take steps to improve tax collection (on the latter issue, see below).

Notwithstanding the legitimate need to enhance tax revenue and collection, it is imperative that well-designed programmes of public expenditure not be frustrated by an obsession with avoiding budget deficits. In this connection, it is difficult to imagine industrialized countries maintaining the kind of fiscal restraint expected of developing countries these days. Indeed, fiscal deficits in industrialized countries remain quite high despite their significant tax base and tax collection rates. The ratio of the public deficit to GDP between 1991 and 1995 was 8 per cent in Sweden,[14] 3 per cent in Germany, 3.3 per cent in the Netherlands, 2.9 per cent in the USA and 5.6 per cent in the UK (Navarro 2001). The German government, long an advocate of the virtues of fiscal restraint in Europe, was embarrassed by the revelation that the

ratio of its budget deficit to GDP rose to 2.7 per cent in early
2002. And US President George Bush quickly stepped away from
his administration's promise to maintain a balanced budget following the events of 11 September 2001.

> Public investment is neither inferior to nor discouraging of
> private investment.

Neoliberal arguments about the virtues of private investment
over the evils of public investment do not stand up to scrutiny.
Neither form of investment is inherently good or bad from the
perspective of development. The productivity of any investment
(in terms of economic growth and social goals) depends on numerous factors, such as the availability of resources, the quality of
the economy's strategic plans, and so on. Nevertheless, the private
sector cannot and should not be expected to initiate projects that
are more appropriately left in the hands of the government (such
as investments in infrastructure).

There is no empirical basis for the neoliberal claim that private
investment is superior to public investment. Private investment is
as prone to political distortions, waste and insider dealing as is
public investment. Similarly, both private and public investment can
involve perverse incentives. This possibility is especially apparent
in the case of public assistance to failed businesses. Neoliberals
usually assail bail-outs of state-owned or quasi-public enterprises
on the ground that they encourage poor business management.
But some large private firms also receive government bail-outs
when they fail. And these bail-outs, too, can introduce perverse
incentives.

Finally, the logical basis for the crowding-out argument is extremely weak, though it does have a powerful ideological appeal
for neoliberals. It is not clear how or why the private sector in
developing countries would be crowded out by public investment,
if the level of private investment is so low in the first place. It
is far more likely that public investment will have a 'crowding in'
or encouraging effect on private investment. Public investment in

education, health, infrastructure, technology and communications are clear pre- or co-requisites for private investment.

It is worth remembering that neoliberals excoriate government borrowing on the ground that it causes domestic interest rates to rise, thereby crowding out private investment. But curiously they are not concerned about the possibility that the high interest rates associated with the domestic financial liberalization programmes that they endorse will crowd out private investment (see also Chapter 10).

Rejection of the neoliberal view of revenue policy

> Neoliberals accept the need for better tax collection, but place far less emphasis on it than on expenditure cuts.

As noted earlier, neoliberals have recently begun to acknowledge the problem of tax collection in developing countries. Clearly, governments in developing countries would have a greater pool of resources at their disposal if they increased tax collection and reduced the opportunities for tax evasion by individuals and firms. However, neoliberals fail to take on the problems associated with tax collection with the same zeal that they devote to promoting expenditure reduction and fiscal balance. Government budget constraints would have far less force if the IMF and national governments invested significant resources in increasing tax collection and reducing the opportunity of powerful actors to evade tax obligations. Increased tax collection would enhance the resources available for public expenditure, and make it less likely that new borrowing would be necessary to finance new expenditure.

Policy alternatives with regard to expenditure policy

> Sustained economic growth and social improvement depend on strategic, well-designed and well-managed increases in government expenditure.

The obsession with fiscal restraint (and, even more so, with budget balance) is clearly inappropriate in the context of economies that have vast social ills and low or even negative rates of economic growth. Developing countries cannot afford excessive fiscal restraint and have no reason to focus on budget balance as a key policy objective in its own right.

Cross-country and historical experience shows that strategic, well-designed and well-managed programmes of public expenditure are critical to the promotion of economic growth, investment and the alleviation of important social ills. Evidence shows, for example, that expenditures on health services and primary education reduce poverty and promote economic growth. Moreover, studies find that public investment in transportation and communications is strongly correlated with economic growth (Easterly and Rebelo 1993). The experience of numerous industrialized countries – let alone the East Asian NICs – underscores the importance of government expenditure on industry, agriculture, infrastructure, and social and educational programmes (see also Chapters 7.1–7.2 and 9.4).

Policy alternatives with regard to revenue policy

> Increases in public expenditure must be tied to the generation of additional tax revenue and a reduction in tax evasion.

Clearly, a programme of growth-promoting public investment and ameliorative social expenditure necessitates at least some increase in tax collection and revenue. There are several avenues that can be explored.

The first avenue involves examining more carefully the revenue implications of various economic policy changes, such as trade and financial liberalization. These changes should not be pursued so long as the tax revenues lost cannot be replaced by other means. Additionally, the tax holidays granted to foreign TNCs (especially those that operate in EPZs) deserve serious examination in light of their costs to the tax base (see Chapter 9.4).

The second avenue involves reducing the opportunities for tax evasion. Domestic residents (especially the wealthy) often evade domestic tax obligations by engaging in capital flight. In this connection, capital controls that are supported by foreign banks and multilateral institutions could reduce the negative effect of capital flight on the tax base (see Chapter 9.2–9.3). It is equally important to curtail the methods for tax evasion that are frequently employed by both domestic- and foreign-owned firms. TNCs deserve special mention in this regard because they have proven especially adept at evading taxes by engaging in transfer pricing that lets them pay taxes in low-tax countries (see Chapter 9.4). The employment and other benefits generated by TNCs must be weighed against the tax costs that they impose on host economies.

The third avenue for increasing tax revenues involves redesigning the VAT so that income taxes are replaced with a *progressive* VAT (Toye 2000). Evidence shows that VAT systems are more 'revenue productive' than are income-based tax systems because they are more difficult to evade. This greater revenue productivity could go a long way towards eliminating the constraints on public expenditure that stem from difficulties with tax collection in developing countries.[15] Although neoliberals also argue for an increased role for VATs, this proposal differs from theirs in that we argue for a 'progressive' VAT that exempts purchases of basic needs and wage goods and imposes a heavy tax on the purchase of luxury goods (Toye, 2000).

The fourth avenue for raising additional tax revenue involves introducing taxes on financial speculation, including taxes on trading in foreign currencies, stock transfers, and short-term international private capital flows (see Chapter 9.2–9.3).[16] National tax authorities could collect taxes on stock transfers and on short-term international capital flows; international bodies, such as the UN, could collect taxes on currency speculation and redistribute the proceeds of such taxes to developing countries (or use them to finance important global development programmes). Nissanke (2003) finds that the introduction of a tax on global currency trading has the potential to raise substantial revenues (while also reducing financial volatility). For instance, she presents revenue forecasts that estimate that taxes on global currency speculation could raise between US$17 and US$35 billion annually.[17] Taxes on speculation have the virtue of being progressive taxes in so far as the poor are not involved in the trading of financial assets.

Notes

1. Note that there are different varieties of floating and pegged rate regimes. For example, floating regimes involve different degrees of central bank intervention in currency markets. What is technically called an independently floating regime most closely approximates a textbook vision of a market-determined exchange rate in so far as intervention in currency markets is minimal. A managed float refers to a situation wherein the central bank intervenes in the exchange market (though it is not committed to maintaining a specific exchange rate or range for the currency). The figure given above is for countries with independent *and* managed floats.

   There is some controversy surrounding the identification of exchange rate regimes in developing countries. This controversy stems from the fact that governments (and even the IMF) often identify certain regimes as floating when in fact the government is known to manage the exchange rate aggressively and surreptitiously (see Calvo and Reinhart 2002).

2. The corner solution idea is widely held among neoliberals today (e.g. Fischer 2001). However, there are a few neoliberals that reject the idea of corner solutions. E.g. Williamson 2002 advances a persuasive defence of intermediate regimes.

3. The Chinese currency has been convertible on the current account since December 1996. Currencies in Western Europe and Japan were convertible only on the current account for much of the post-World War II era.

4. In the currency futures market, an individual or firm can purchase the promise that a specific amount of foreign currency will be delivered on a particular date in the future at a price that is agreed upon today.

5. The Indian currency became convertible on the current account in 1994.

6. The objective of this type of selective currency convertibility can also be achieved by dual exchange rate regimes. Both seek to protect the tradable goods sector from the currency instability engendered by currency speculation.

7. Recent empirical work by Williamson (2002) provides additional support for pegged exchange rate regimes in developing countries. He finds that 17 out of 33 episodes of rapid economic growth in developing countries since 1980 were in countries that had some type of pegged rate regime. Williamson defines an episode of rapid growth as the attainment of an annual GDP growth rate of more than 6 per cent for at least three years. Clearly, the evidence presented by Williamson does not prove that pegged exchange rates alone were responsible for these economic growth achievements (and nor does he make this claim).

8. The World Bank study argues that while moderate inflation is not economically costly, it is nevertheless problematic. This is because moderate inflation can lead policymakers to develop a kind of 'inflation habit', a habit that can culminate in costly, high inflation in the future. However, the study provides no evidence for this assertion.

9. In the 1960s, the Korean inflation rate was higher than that of Venezuela (1.3 per cent), Bolivia (3.5 per cent), Mexico (3.6 per cent), Peru (10.4 per cent) and Colombia (11.9 per cent), and was not much lower than that of Argentina (21.7 per cent). In the 1970s, Korea's inflation rate was higher than that of Venezuela (12.1 per cent), Ecuador (14.4 per cent) and Mexico (19.3 per cent), and was not much lower than that in Colombia (22.0 per cent) or Bolivia (22.3 per cent). See Singh 1995: Table 5 for further data.

10. Epstein (2001) proposes employment targets for monetary policy; Kirshner (2000) proposes broadening the goals of monetary policy along the lines suggested here.

11. Note that all of the data referenced in section 11.3 – except where noted – are from Toye 2000.

12. Alan Blinder (1997), prominent US economist and former vice-chair of the Board of Governors of the US Federal Reserve, calls for the creation of independent fiscal authorities in the USA. Eichengreen, Hausmann and Von Hagen (1999) propose the creation of politically accountable National Fiscal Councils in Latin America.

13. Many of the arguments below regarding the composition of expenditure reductions and the contribution of neoliberal reform to fiscal imbalance draw heavily on Toye 2000.

14. This was largely due to a banking crisis that followed neoliberal financial reform in the late 1980s.

15. For example, one study finds that developing countries raised tax revenue that is only equivalent to 3.38 per cent of their GDP through income and social security taxes in the late 1980s. By contrast, industrialized countries raised tax revenue equivalent to 17.35 per cent of their GDP through income and social security taxes during the same period (Toye 2000).

16. A tax on currency speculation is commonly referred to as the Tobin Tax. The tax is named for Nobel laureate economist James Tobin, who first proposed it in a paper published in 1974.

17. See Grabel 2003d for estimates of the revenue potential from other types of speculation tax.

Conclusion

Obstacles and Opportunities
for Reclaiming Development

In the preceding chapters we have explored the faulty foundations of the neoliberal development agenda. We have seen that the case for neoliberal economic policies is based on weak theoretical, empirical, institutional and/or historical grounds. By contrast, we have shown that myriad alternatives in critical domains of economic policy are available that can be employed in the service of more rapid, equitable, stable and sustainable development. The latter include trade, industry, privatization, intellectual property rights, foreign bank borrowing, portfolio and foreign direct investment, domestic financial regulation, exchange rates and currencies, central banking and monetary policy, and government revenue and expenditure. Through this work we hope to have defeated the triumphalism that has surrounded the neoliberal agenda for the past twenty-five years.

In our exploration of policy alternatives, we have argued that the appropriateness of any particular policy depends on specific national conditions, such as resource endowments, the scarcity of foreign exchange, proximity to key markets, social and political conditions, and so on. Where possible, we have provided guidance as to the types of policies that might be best suited to particular country conditions.

Finally, we have shown that unlike many aspects of the neoliberal policy agenda, the alternative economic policies that we articulate have a sound basis in economic theory (e.g. see the essays in Chang 2003). In most cases, the need for and viability of alternative economic policies are supported by historical evidence relating to the development strategies and trajectories of today's wealthy countries, and/or by the recent experience of several developing countries. Of course, no track record can be invoked in support of the policies we advance that are more innovative or experimental in nature. But we maintain that the vast challenges facing developing countries today make it all the more important that policymakers think more creatively about policy options.

We are well aware that even our most sympathetic readers might respond to this book by reminding us that the changing rules of the global economy over the last quarter of a century have made some of the alternative policies that we discuss difficult (or even impossible) to implement in developing countries. The sceptical reader would rightly invoke the pressures for neoliberal policy that emanate from the IMF, the World Bank and the WTO, various international agreements such as free-trade agreements, donor governments, private international lenders, and the domestic and international investment community. We certainly do not deny the severe constraints that these actors have introduced in the developing world. *However, we maintain that it is both fatalistic and incorrect to act as if their power and influence are absolute and immutable.* If so, then surely there is little hope for today's developing countries.

In our view, it is imperative that advocates of alternative economic policies not take the rules of the current global environment as fixed. It is always possible, and is certainly necessary, to rewrite the global rules. We realize that this is not easy, especially in a world dominated by an increasingly unilateralist US government. However, rewriting the rules should not be seen as an impossible task. By now, long-standing critics of neoliberal policy in the developing world (and elsewhere) have a vast arsenal of evidence to support their case against this failed policy regime. We are encouraged by the number and strength of new cross-border social movements opposed to neoliberal, corporate-led globalization and anti-democratic multilateral institutions and agreements. We certainly hope that our work contributes to conversation among policymakers and activists about positive alternatives to neoliberal policy.

At the present juncture, long-standing critics of neoliberal policy may find that they share some common ground with those who have recently become disillusioned with certain aspects of the neoliberal agenda. For example, it is now fairly uncontroversial that developing economies should be protected from the financial crises that often follow the liberalization of capital flows; that privatization programmes should not simply transfer resources from one group of insiders to another; and that tax evasion is at least as important as expenditure reduction in the face of budget deficits. These areas of agreement can and should be exploited in discussions of policy whenever possible.

It is equally important to acknowledge that many of the alternative policies that we discuss can be employed *even without radical changes in the global environment*. A great many of the policies that we discuss in Part II have been employed successfully (and without penalty from international investors or lenders) in the recent past or are still in use today in some countries. For example, many (but not all) of the strategies towards trade, industry and intellectual property rights that we discuss are not specifically prohibited by the WTO today. The same can be said about the IMF in relation to at least a number of the financial, investment and currency policies that we present. It is also the case that a country's policymakers may find it possible to combine neoliberal policy in some part of the economy with alternative policies in other domains. For instance, policymakers in small, poor countries might establish a free-trade zone that welcomes unregulated foreign direct investment in certain industries in order to earn foreign exchange, while simultaneously pursuing restrictive policies over FDI in other sectors of the economy in order to promote technological advance (see, e.g., Chapter 9.4).

Policymakers across developing countries can also work collectively to increase their ability to pursue alternative economic policies. In this connection, regionalism and/or bilateral economic agreements among developing countries can be an important way to increase bargaining power vis-à-vis external actors, especially in the case of very poor and/or very small countries (DeMartino 1999). Moreover, policy coordination across developing countries might reduce the costs and risks of policy experimentation. For instance, the coordinated use of capital controls might reduce financial instability with the effect of increasing capital flows to all developing countries (Grabel 2003a). In this connection, larger developing countries that have had positive experience with alternative policies have an important leadership role to play in advocating for new regimes.

The hope for more rapid, equitable, stable and sustainable development has been too long deferred by economists and policymakers who are so wedded to the neoliberal orthodoxy that they can neither imagine nor countenance any alternative. They have pursued the neoliberal agenda with extraordinary single-mindedness and even hubris. The effect has been devastating: in the wake of the neoliberal experiment, we find extraordinary misery, inequality and despair on a scale unknown in recent human history.

Fortunately, Margaret Thatcher was wrong. There are alternatives – an abundance of alternatives, in fact – that can begin to make good on the promises of economic development. We have presented a good many of these alternatives here, in the hope of solidifying this claim.

Surely the need to 'Reclaim Development' has never been more pressing. We offer this book as a small contribution to that task.

References

Amsden, A. (1989) *Asia's Next Giant*, New York: Oxford University Press.

Arestis, P. and P. Demetriades (1997) 'Financial development and economic growth: Assessing the evidence', *Economic Journal* 107(442): 783–99.

Ariyoshi, A., K. Habermeier, B. Laurens, I. Otker-Robe, J. Canales-Kriljenko and A. Kirilenko (2000) *County Experience with the Use and Liberalization of Capital Controls*, Washington DC: IMF.

Atkinson, A. (2002) 'Top incomes in the united kingdom over the twentieth century', mimeo, Nuffield College, Oxford.

Bird, G. and R. Ramkishen (2001) 'International currency taxation and currency stabilisation in developing countries', *Journal of Development Studies* 37(3): 21–38.

Baker, D. (2000) 'Something new in the 1990s? Looking for evidence of an economic transformation', in J. Madrick (ed.), *Unconventional Wisdom: Alternative Perspectives on the New Economy*, New York: Century Foundation Press.

—— (2002) '*Business Week* restates the 1990s – Incorrectly?', *Challenge* (45)4, August: 122–8.

Barro, R. (1996) 'Inflation and growth', *Review of Federal Reserve Bank of St. Louis* 78: 153–69.

Berger, A., N. Miller, M. Petersen, R. Raajan, and J. Stein (2001) 'Does function follow organizational form? Evidence from the lending practices of large and small banks', NBER paper, December.

Berger, S. and R. Dore (eds) (1996) *National Diversity and Global Capitalism*, Ithaca: Cornell University Press.

Blinder, A. (1997) 'Is government too political?', *Foreign Affairs* 76(6) 115–27.

Bogetic, Z., (2000) 'Full dollarization: Fad or future?', *Challenge* 43(2): 17–48.

Brittan, L. (1995) 'Investment liberalisation: The next great boost to the world economy', *Transnational Corporations* 4(1).

Bruno, M. (1995) 'Does inflation really lower growth?', *Finance and Development* 32(3), September: 35–8.

——— and W. Easterly (1996) 'Inflation and growth: In search of a stable relationship', *Review of Federal Reserve Bank of St. Louis*, May/June: 139–46.

Calvo, G. and C. Reinhart (2002) 'Fear of floating?', *Quarterly Journal of Economics* 117(2): 379–408.

Chang, H.-J. (1994) *The Political Economy of Industrial Policy*, London: Macmillan.

——— (2001) 'Rethinking East Asian industrial policy – Past records and future prospects', in P.-K. Wong and C-Y. Ng (eds), *Industrial Policy, Innovation and Economic Growth*, Singapore: Singapore University Press.

——— (2002) *Kicking Away the Ladder*, London: Anthem Press.

——— (ed.) (2003), *Rethinking Development Economics*, London: Anthem Press.

——— and D. Green (2003) 'The Northern WTO Agenda on Investment: Do as we say, not as we did', London and Geneva, South Centre–CAFOD (Catholic Agency for Overseas Development) joint working paper, June.

Clements, B., S. Gupta and J. Schiff (1996) 'Worldwide military spending, 1990–95', IMF Working Paper No. 96/64, June.

Cohen, S. (1977) *Modern Capitalist Planning: The French Model*, Berkeley: University of California Press.

Cornia, G. A. (2003) 'Globalisation and the distribution of income between and within countries', in H.-J. Chang (ed.) *Rethinking Development Economics*, London: Anthem Press.

DeMartino, G. (1999) 'Global neoliberalism, policy autonomy, and international competitive dynamics', *Journal of Economic Issues* 33(2): 343–9.

——— (2000) *Global Economy, Global Justice: Theoretical Objections and Policy Alternatives to Neoliberalism*, London: Routledge.

Demirgüc-Kunt, A. and E. Detragiache (1998) 'Financial liberalization and financial fragility', International Monetary Fund Working Paper No. 83.

Dodd, R. (2000) 'The role of derivatives in the East Asian crisis', Derivatives Study Center, Washington DC, unpublished paper.

Easterly, W. and S. Rebelo (1993) 'Fiscal policy and economic growth', *Journal of Monetary Economics* 32: 417–58.

Economic Commission for Latin America and the Caribbean (ECLAC) (2002) *Globalization and Development*, Santiago: ECLAC/CEPAL.

Economic Report of the President (ERP) (2001), 107th Congress, 1st session, Washington DC: US Government Printing Office.

Eichengreen, B., R. Hausmann, J. Von Hagen (1999) 'Reforming budgetary institutions in Latin America', *Open Economies Review* 10: 415–22.

Eijffinger S. and J. de Haan (1996) 'The political economy of central-bank independence', *Special Papers in International Economics*, No. 19, Princeton University.

Eichengreen, Barry (2001) 'Capital account liberalization: What do cross-country studies tell us?', *World Bank Economic Review* 15(3): 341–65.

Epstein, G. (2001) 'Financialization, rentier interests, and central bank policy', Department of Economics, University of Massachusetts–Amherst, unpublished paper.

——— I. Grabel and K.S. Jomo (2003) 'Capital management techniques in developing countries: An assessment of experiences from the 1990's and lessons for the future', in A. Buira (ed.), *Challenges to the World Bank and IMF*, London: Anthem Press.

Evans, D. (1989) *Comparative Advantage and Growth*, New York: Harvester Wheatsheaf.

Evans, P. (1987) 'Class, state, and dependence in East Asia: Lessons for Latin Americanists', in F. Deyo (ed.), *The Political Economy of the New Asian Industrialism*, Ithaca: Cornell University Press.

Financial Times (2001) 'Strong global patent rules increase the cost of medicines', 14 February: 20.

Fischer, S. (2001) 'Exchange rate regimes: Is the bipolar view correct?', *Journal of Economic Perspectives* 15(2): 3–24.

Gerschenkron, A. (1962) *Economic Backwardness in Historical Perspective*, Cambridge MA: Harvard University Press.

Grabel, I. (1995) 'Speculation-led economic development: A post-Keynesian interpretation of financial liberalization in the Third World', *International Review of Applied Economics* 9(2): 127–49.

——— (1996) 'Marketing the third world: The contradictions of portfolio investment in the global economy', *World Development* 24(11): 1761–76.

——— (1997) 'Savings, investment and functional efficiency: A comparative examination of national financial complexes', in R. Pollin (ed.), *The Macroeconomics of Finance, Saving, and Investment*, Ann Arbor: University of Michigan Press, 251–97.

———— (2000) 'The political economy of "Policy Credibility": The new-classical macroeconomics and the remaking of emerging economies', *Cambridge Journal of Economics* 24(1): 1–19.

———— (2002) 'Neoliberal finance and crisis in the developing world', *Monthly Review* 53(11), April: 34–46.

———— (2003a) 'Averting crisis: Assessing measures to manage financial integration in emerging economies', *Cambridge Journal of Economics* 27(3): 317–36.

———— (2003b) 'Predicting financial crisis in developing economies: Astronomy or astrology?', *Eastern Economics Journal* 29(2): 245–60.

———— (2003c) 'Ideology, power and the rise of independent monetary institutions in emerging economies', in J. Kirshner (ed.) *Monetary Orders: Ambiguous Economics, Ubiquitous Politics*, Ithaca: Cornell University Press, 25–52.

———— (2003d) 'The reserve and double dividend potential of taxes on international private capital flows and securities transactions', World Institute for Development Economics Research (WIDER), Discussion paper No. 2003/83.

———— (2004) 'Trip wires and speed bumps: Managing financial risks and reducing the potential for financial crises in developing economies', paper prepared for the XVIIIth Technical Group Meeting of the Group of Twenty-Four, Geneva, 8–9 March.

Grieve-Smith, J. (2002) 'Exchange rates management', paper prepared for the conference of the coalition for 'New Rules for Global Finance, 23–24 May 2002, www.new-rules.org/Conference/conference.html.

Held, D., A. McGrew, D. Goldblatt and J. Perraton (1999) *Global Transformation*, Cambridge: Polity Press.

Helleiner, E. (1994) *States and Reemergence of Global Finance*, Ithaca, NY: Cornell University Press.

Johnson, C. (1982) *MITI and the Japanese Miracle*, Stanford: Stanford University Press.

Julius, D. (1994) 'International direct investment: Strengthening the policy regime', in G. Kenen (ed.), *Managing the World Economy*, Washington DC: Institute for International Economics.

Kaplan, E. and D. Rodrik (2001) 'Did the Malaysian capital controls work?', in S. Edwards and J. Frankel (eds) *Preventing Currency Crises in Emerging Markets*, Chicago: University of Chicago Press, 393–441.

Kirshner, J. (2000) 'The political economy of low inflation', *Journal of Economic Surveys* 15(1): 41–70.

Krueger, A. (1980) 'Trade policy as an input to development', *American Economic Review* 70(2).

Krugman, P. (ed.) (1988) *Strategic Trade Policy and the New International Economics*, Cambridge MA: MIT Press.

—— (2002) 'For richer', *New York Times*, 20 October, 62–7, 75–7, 141–2.

Kuczynski, P.-P. and J. Williamson (eds) (2003) *After the Washington Consensus* Washington DC: Institute for International Economics.

Levin, R., A. Klevorick, R. Nelson and S. Winter (1987) 'Appropriating the returns from industrial research and development', *Brookings Papers on Economic Activity*, No. 3.

Little, I., T. Scitovsky and M. Scott (1970) *Industry and Trade in Some Developing Countries – A Comparative Study*, London: Oxford University Press.

Machlup, F. and E. Penrose (1951) 'The patent controversy in the nineteenth century', *Journal of Economic History* 10(1).

Maddison, A. (1989) *The World Economy in the Twentieth Century*, Paris: OECD.

Mas, I. (1995) 'Central bank independence: A critical view from a developing country perspective', *World Development* 23(10): 1639–52.

Maxfield, S. (1997) *Gatekeepers of Growth*, Princeton: Princeton University Press.

Milberg, W. (1998) 'Globalisation', in R. Kozul-Wright and R. Rowthorn (eds), *Transnational Corporations and the World Economy*, London: Macmillan.

Mowery, D. and Rosenberg, N. (1993) 'The US national innovation system', in R. Nelson (ed.), *National Innovation Systems – A Comparative Analysis*, Oxford: Oxford University Press.

National Law Centre for Inter-American Free Trade (1997) 'Strong intellectual property protection benefits the developing countries', www.natlaw.com/pubs/spmxip11.htm.

Navarro, V. (2001) 'The end of full-employment and expansionist policies?', *Challenge* 44(5): 19–29.

New York Times (2002) 'Gains of 90s did not lift all, census shows', 5 June, A1, A20.

Nissanke, M. (2003) 'The revenue potential of the currency transaction tax for development finance', World Institute for Development Economics Research (WIDER), Discussion Paper No. 2003/81.

Odagiri, H. and A. Goto (1993) 'The Japanese system of innovation', in R. Nelson (ed.), *National Innovation Systems – A Comparative Analysis*, Oxford: Oxford University Press.

O'Rourke, K. and J. Williamson (1999) *Globalization and History: The Evolution of Nineteenth-Century Atlantic Economy*, Cambridge MA: MIT Press.

Palast, G. (2000) 'Keep taking our tablets (no one else's)', *Observer*, 23 July, Business Section, 7.

Palley, T. (2000) 'Stabilizing finance: The case for asset-based reserve requirements', *Financial Markets and Society*, August.

Palma, G. (2000) 'The three routes to financial crises: The need for capital controls', CEPA Working Paper Series III, No. 18, New School University, New York.

Pilling, D. (2001) 'Patents and patients', *Financial Times*, 17–18 February.

Prasad, E., K. Rogoff, S.-J. Wei and M. Kose (2003) 'Effects of financial globalization on developing countries: Some empirical evidence', www.imf.org/external/np/res/docs/2003/031703.htm.

Rodriguez, F. and D. Rodrik (2001) 'Trade policy and economic growth – A skeptic's guide to the cross-national evidence', *NBER Macroeconomics Annual 2000*, Cambridge MA: MIT Press.

Rodrik, D. (1998) 'Who needs capital-account convertibility?', in P. Kenen (ed.), *Should the IMF Pursue Capital-Account Convertibility*, Princeton Essays in International Finance, No. 207, 55–65.

——— (2002) 'After neoliberalism, what?', paper presented at 'Alternatives to Neoliberalism', a conference of the Coalition for 'New Rules for Global Finance', 22–23 May, Washington DC.

RAFI (Rural Advancement Foundation International) (2000) RAFI Communique 66, September/October.

Sachs, J. and A. Warner (1995) 'Economic reform and the process of global integration', *Brookings Papers on Economic Activity*, No. 1.

Schiff, E. (1971) *Industrialisation without National Patents: The Netherlands, 1869–1912 and Switzerland, 1850–1907*, Princeton: Princeton University Press.

Sikken, B. and J. de Haan (1998) 'Budget deficits, monetization, and central-bank independence in developing countries', *Oxford Economic Papers* 50: 493–511.

Singh, A. (1995) 'How did East Asia grow so fast? – Slow progress towards an analytical consensus', UNCTAD Discussion Paper No. 97, Geneva, United Nations Conference on Trade and Development (UNCTAD).

——— and B. Weisse (1998) 'Emerging stock markets, portfolio capital flows and long-term economic growth: Micro and macroeconomic perspectives', *World Development* 26(4): 607–22.

Standgate, T. (1999) *The Victorian Internet*, London: Phoenix.

Tobin, J. (1984) 'On the efficiency of the financial system', *Lloyds Bank Review* 153: 1–15

Toye, J. (2000) 'Fiscal crisis and fiscal reform in developing countries', *Cambridge Journal of Economics* 24(1): 21–44.

United Nations Development Program (UNDP) (various years) *Human Development Report*, Oxford: Oxford University Press.

Vaitsos, C. (1972) 'Patent revisited: Their function in developing countries', *Journal of Development Studies* 9(1).

Velde, F. and M. Veracierto (2000) 'Dollarization in Argentina', *Federal Reserve Bank of Chicago Economic Perspective*, First Quarter: 24–35.

Wade, R. (1990) *Governing the Market*, Princeton: Princeton University Press.

Weisbrot, M., D. Baker, E. Kraev and J. Chen (2001) 'The scorecard on globalization 1980–2000', Center for Economic Policy Research, September, www.cepr.net/globalization/scorecard_on_globalization. htm.

Weller, C. (2001) 'Financial crises after financial liberalisation: Exceptional circumstances or structural weakness?', *Journal of Development Studies* 38(1): 98–127.

———— and A. Hersh (2002) 'The long and short of it: Global liberalization, poverty and inequality', Economic Policy Institute, Washington DC, unpublished paper.

Williamson, J. (2002) *Exchange Rate Regimes for Emerging Markets: Reviving the Intermediate Option*, Washington DC: Institute for International Economics.

———— and M. Mahar (1998) 'A survey of financial liberalization', *Princeton Essays in International Finance*, No. 211, November.

Wolff, E.N. (2000) 'Why stocks won't save the middle class', in J. Madrick (ed.), *Unconventional Wisdom: Alternative Perspectives on the New Economy*, New York: Century Foundation Press.

Woo-Cumings, M. (ed.) (1999) *The Developmental State*, Ithaca: Cornell University Press.

World Bank (1985) *World Development Report 1985*, New York: Oxford University Press.

———— (1995) *Bureaucrats in Business*, New York: Oxford University Press.

———— (2002) *World Development Report 2002*, Oxford: Oxford University Press.

———— (various years) *Global Development Finance*, Washington DC: World Bank.

Recommended Further Reading

7.1 Neoliberal

Bhagwati, J. (1985) *Protectionism*, Cambridge MA: MIT Press.

World Bank (1987) *World Development Report 1987*, New York: Oxford University Press.

Alternative

Chang, H.-J. (2002) *Kicking Away the Ladder – Development Strategy in Historical Perspective*, London: Anthem Press, ch. 2.

Helleiner, G. (1990) Trade strategy in medium-term adjustment', *World Development* 18(6).

7.2 Neoliberal

Lindbeck, A. (1981) 'Industrial policy as an issue in the economic environment, *The World Economy* 4(4).

World Bank (1993) *East Asian Miracle*, New York: Oxford University Press.

Alternative

Amsden, A. (1989) *Asia's Next Giant*, New York: Oxford University Press.

Chang, H.-J. (1994) *The Political Economy of Industrial Policy*, London: Macmillan.

8.1 Neoliberal

World Bank (1983) *World Development Report 1983*, Part I, esp. chs 4–8.

World Bank (1995) *Bureaucrats in Business*, New York: Oxford University Press.

Alternative

Chang, H.-J. and A. Singh (1993) 'Public enterprises in developing countries and economic efficiency', *UNCTAD Review* 4; shortened version reprinted in H.-J. Chang (2003), *Globalization, Economic Development and the Role of the State*, London: Zed Books.

Cook, P. and C. Kirkpatrick (eds) (1988) *Privatisation in Less Developed Countries*, Brighton: Harvester Wheatsheaf.

8.2 Neoliberal

Primo Braga, C. (1996) 'Trade-related intellectual property issues: The Uruguay round agreement and its economic implications', in W. Martin and A. Winters (eds), *The Uruguay Round and the Developing Countries*, Cambridge: Cambridge University Press.

National Law Centre for Inter-American Free Trade (1997) 'Strong intellectual property protection benefits the developing countries', www.natlaw.com/pubs/spmxip11.htm.

Alternative

Chang, H-J. (2001) 'Intellectual property rights and economic development: Historical lessons and emerging issues', *Journal of Human Development* 2(2).

UNDP (1999) *Human Development Report 1999*, New York: Oxford University Press.

9.1 Neoliberal

International Finance Corporation (IFC) *Emerging Stock Markets Factbook*, Washington DC: IFC, various years.

International Monetary Fund (IMF), *Annual Report on Exchange Restrictions*, Washington DC: IMF, various years.

Alternative

Grabel, I. (2003) 'International private capital flows and developing countries', in H.-J. Chang (ed.), *Rethinking Development Economics*, London: Anthem Press, 325–45.

9.2 Neoliberal

Cline, W. (1995), *International Debt Reexamined*, Washington DC: Institute for International Economics.

Alternative

George, S. (1990) *A Fate Worse than Debt: The World Financial Crisis and the Poor*, London: Pluto Press.

Payer, C. (1991) *Lent and Lost*, London: Zed Books.

9.3 Neoliberal

Edwards, S. (1999) 'How effective are capital controls?', *Journal of Economic Perspectives* 13(4).

———— (2001) 'Capital mobility and economic performance: Are emerging economies different?', National Bureau of Economic Research Working Paper 8076.

Alternative

Ffrench-Davis, R. and H. Reisen (eds) (1998) *Capital Flows and Investment Performance*, Paris: ECLAC Development Centre and OECD.

United Nations Conference on Trade and Economic Development (UNCTAD) (1997) *International Monetary and Financial Issues for the 1990s*, Research papers from the Group of Twenty-four, vol. 8.

9.4 Neoliberal

Julius, D. (1994) 'International direct investment: Strengthening the policy regime', in G. Kenen (ed.), *Managing the World Economy*, Washington DC: Institute for International Economics.

UNCTAD, *World Investment Report*, various years, New York: UNCTAD.

Alternative

Chang, H.-J. (1998), 'Globalisation, transnational corporations, and economic development', in D. Baker, G. Epstein and R. Pollin (eds), *Globalisation and Progressive Economic Policy*, Cambridge: Cambridge University Press.

Helleiner, G. (1989) 'Transnational corporations and direct foreign investment', in H. Chenery and T.N. Srinivasan (eds), *Handbook of Development Economics*, vol. 2, Amsterdam: Elsevier.

10 Neoliberal

Fry, M. (1995) *Money, Interest, and Banking in Economic Development*, Baltimore: Johns Hopkins University Press.

Levine, R. (1997) 'Financial development and economic growth: Views and agenda', *Journal of Economic Literature* 35: 688–726.

Alternative

Brownbridge, M. and C. Kirkpatrick (2000) 'Financial regulation in developing countries' *Journal of Development Studies* 37(1): 1–24.

Diaz-Alejandro, C. (1985) 'Good-bye financial repression, hello financial crash', *Journal of Development Economics* 19: 1–24.

11.1 Neoliberal

Deepak L. (2001) 'Convertibility and the Asian crisis', in W. Mahmud (ed.), *Adjustment and Beyond*, London: Palgrave, 318–21.

Hanke, S. and K. Schuler (1994) *Currency Boards for Developing Countries*, San Francisco: International Center for Economic Growth.

LeBaron, B. and R. McCulloch (2000) 'Floating, fixed or super-fixed? Dollarization joins the menu of exchange-rate options', *American Economics Review* 90(2): 32–7.

Alternative

Joshi, V. (2001) 'Capital controls and the national advantage: India in the 1990s and beyond', *Oxford Development Studies* 29(3).

Sachs, J. and F. Larrain (1999) 'Why dollarization is more straightjacket than salvation', *Foreign Policy*: 81–92.

11.2 Neoliberal

Meyers, J. (2001) 'Inflation targets and inflation targeting', *Federal Reserve Bank of St. Louis* 83(6): 1–14.

Alternative

Bowles, P. and G. White (1994) 'Central bank independence: A political economy approach', *Journal of Development Studies* 31(2): 235–64.

de Carvalho, C. (1995–6) 'The independence of central banks: A critical assessment of the arguments', *Journal of Post-Keynesian Economics* 18(2): 159–75.

Grabel, I. (2000) 'The political economy of "policy credibility": The new-classical macroeconomics and the remaking of emerging economies', *Cambridge Journal of Economics* 24(1): 1–19.

11.3 Neoliberal

Poterba, J. and J. von Hagen (eds) (1999) *Fiscal Institutions and Fiscal Performance*, Chicago: University of Chicago Press.

Alternative

Rudra, N. (2002) 'Globalization and the decline of the welfare state in less-developed countries' *International Organization* 56(2): 411–45.

Toye, J. and C. Jackson (1996) 'Public expenditure policy and poverty reduction: Has the World Bank got it right?' *IDS Bulletin* 27(1).

Index

About the Authors

Dr Ha-Joon Chang is Assistant Director of Development Studies in the Faculty of Economics and Politics, University of Cambridge. Born in the Republic of Korea, and educated at the Seoul National University and subsequently at Cambridge, he is the author of *The Political Economy of Industrial Policy* (Macmillan, 1994), *Kicking Away the Ladder: Development Strategy in Historical Perspective* (Anthem, 2002); *Globalization, Economic Development, and the Role of the State* (Zed, 2003), and *Restructuring Korea Inc.* (RoutledgeCurzon, 2003; with Jang-Sup Shin); editor of seven other volumes, and has written numerous scholarly journal articles. Since 1992 he has also served on the editorial board of the *Cambridge Journal of Economics*. He was a member of the Advisory Panel for the *Human Development Report 1999* and has acted as research project coordinator and consultant to numerous UN agencies and international agencies including the World Bank, the Asian Development Bank, the British Government's DfID, the Canadian Government's IDRC, and the South Centre in Geneva.

Dr Ilene Grabel is Associate Professor and Co-Director of the graduate programme in Global Finance, Trade and Economic Integration at the University of Denver's Graduate School of International Studies. She also lectures at the Cambridge University Advanced Programme on Rethinking Development Economics. She has published widely in academic journals on financial policy and crises, international capital flows, and central banks and currency boards. She has been a consultant to the UN/UNCTAD Group of Twenty-Four and the UN University's World Institute for Development Economics Research (WIDER) and works with the international NGO coalition New Rules for Global Finance.

A Brave New Series

Global Issues in a Changing World

This new series of short, accessible think-pieces deals with leading global issues of relevance to humanity today. Intended for the enquiring reader and social activists in the North and the South, as well as students, the books explain what is at stake and question conventional ideas and policies. Drawn from many different parts of the world, the series' authors pay particular attention to the needs and interests of ordinary people, whether living in the rich industrial or the developing countries. They all share a common objective – to help stimulate new thinking and social action in the opening years of the new century.

Global Issues in a Changing World is a joint initiative by Zed Books in collaboration with a number of partner publishers and non-governmental organizations around the world. By working together, we intend to maximize the relevance and availability of the books published in the series.

Participating NGOs

Both ENDS, Amsterdam
Catholic Institute for International Relations, London
Corner House, Sturminster Newton
Council on International and Public Affairs, New York
Dag Hammarskjöld Foundation, Uppsala
Development GAP, Washington DC
Focus on the Global South, Bangkok
IBON, Manila
Inter Pares, Ottawa
Public Interest Research Centre, Delhi
Third World Network, Penang
Third World Network–Africa, Accra
World Development Movement, London

About this Series

'Communities in the South are facing great difficulties in coping with global trends. I hope this brave new series will throw much needed light on the issues ahead and help us choose the right options.'

Martin Khor, Director,
Third World Network, Penang

'There is no more important campaign than our struggle to bring the global economy under democratic control. But the issues are fearsomely complex. This Global Issues series is a valuable resource for the committed campaigner and the educated citizen.'

Barry Coates, Director,
World Development Movement (WDM)

'Zed Books has long provided an inspiring list about the issues that touch and change people's lives. The Global Issues series is another dimension of Zed's fine record, allowing access to a range of subjects and authors that, to my knowledge, very few publishers have tried. I strongly recommend these new, powerful titles and this exciting series.'

John Pilger, author

'We are all part of a generation that actually has the means to eliminate extreme poverty world-wide. Our task is to harness the forces of globalization for the benefit of working people, their families and their communities – that is our collective duty. The Global Issues series makes a powerful contribution to the global campaign for justice, sustainable and equitable development, and peaceful progress.'

Glenys Kinnock, MEP

The Global Issues Series

Already available

In preparation

Peggy Antrobus, *The International Women's Movement: Issues and Strategies*

Julian Burger, *First Peoples: What Future?*

Koen de Feyter, *A Thousand and One Rights: How Globalization Challenges Human Rights*

Susan Hawley and Morris Szeftel, *Corruption: Privatization, Transnational Corporations and the Export of Bribery*

Roger Moody, *Digging the Dirt: The Modern World of Global Mining*

Edgar Pieterse, *City Futures: Confronting the Crisis of Urban Development*

Toby Shelley, *Oil and Gas: What Future? What Consequences?*

Kavaljit Singh, *The Myth of Globalization: Ten Questions Everyone Asks*

Vivien Stern, *Crime and Punishment: Globalization and the New Agenda*

Nedd Willard, *The Drugs War: Is This the Solution?*

For full details of this list and Zed's other subject and general catalogues, please write to: The Marketing Department, Zed Books, 7 Cynthia Street, London N1 9JF, UK or email Sales@zedbooks.demon.co.uk

Visit our website at: www.zedbooks.co.uk

Participating Organizations

Both ENDS A service and advocacy organization which collaborates with environment and indigenous organizations, both in the South and in the North, with the aim of helping to create and sustain a vigilant and effective environmental movement.

> Nieuwe Keizersgracht 45, 1018 VC Amsterdam, The Netherlands
> Phone: +31 20 623 0823   Fax: +31 20 620 8049
> Email: info@bothends.org   Website: www.bothends.org

Catholic Institute for International Relations (CIIR) CIIR aims to contribute to the eradication of poverty through a programme that combines advocacy at national and international level with community-based development.

> Unit 3, Canonbury Yard, 190a New North Road, London N1 7BJ, UK
> Phone +44 (0)20 7354 0883   Fax +44 (0)20 7359 0017
> Email: ciir@ciir.org   Website: www.ciir.org

Corner House The Corner House is a UK-based research and solidarity group working on social and environmental justice issues in North and South.

> PO Box 3137, Station Road, Sturminster Newton, Dorset DT10 1YJ, UK
> Tel.: +44 (0)1258 473795   Fax: +44 (0)1258 473748
> Email: cornerhouse@gn.apc.org   Website: www.cornerhouse.icaap.org

Council on International and Public Affairs (CIPA) CIPA is a human rights research, education and advocacy group, with a particular focus on economic and social rights in the USA and elsewhere around the world. Emphasis in recent years has been given to resistance to corporate domination.

> 777 United Nations Plaza, Suite 3C, New York, NY 10017, USA
> Tel. +1 212 972 9877   Fax +1 212 972 9878
> Email: cipany@igc.org   Website: www.cipa-apex.org

Dag Hammarskjöld Foundation The Dag Hammarskjöld Foundation, established 1962, organises seminars and workshops on social, economic and cultural issues facing developing countries with a particular focus on alternative and innovative solutions. Results are published in its journal *Develpment Dialogue*.

> Övre Slottsgatan 2, 753 10 Uppsala, Sweden.
> Tel.: +46 18 102772   Fax: +46 18 122072
> Email: secretariat@dhf.uu.se   Website: www.dhf.uu.se

Development GAP   The Development Group for Alternative Policies is a Non-Profit Development Resource Organization working with popular organizations in the South and their Northern partners in support of a development that is truly sustainable and that advances social justice.

927 15th Street NW, 4th Floor, Washington, DC, 20005, USA
Tel.: +1 202 898 1566   Fax: +1 202 898 1612
E-mail: dgap@igc.org   Website: www.developmentgap.org

Focus on the Global South   Focus is dedicated to regional and global policy analysis and advocacy work. It works to strengthen the capacity of organizations of the poor and marginalized people of the South and to better analyse and understand the impacts of the globalization process on their daily lives.

C/o CUSRI, Chulalongkorn University, Bangkok 10330, Thailand
Tel.: +66 2 218 7363 Fax: +66 2 255 9976
Email: Admin@focusweb.org   Website: www.focusweb.org

IBON   IBON Foundation is a research, education and information institution that provides publications and services on socio-economic issues as support to advocacy in the Philippines and abroad. Through its research and databank, formal and non-formal education programmes, media work and international networking, IBON aims to build the capacity of both Philippine and international organizations.

Room 303 SCC Bldg, 4427 Int. Old Sta. Mesa, Manila 1008, Philippines
Phone +632 7132729   Fax +632 7160108
Email: editors@ibon.org   Website: www.ibon.org

Inter Pares   Inter Pares, a Canadian social justice organization, has been active since 1975 in building relationships with Third World development groups and providing support for community-based development programs. Inter Pares is also involved in education and advocacy in Canada, promoting understanding about the causes, effects and solutions to poverty.

221 Laurier Avenue East, Ottawa, Ontario, K1N 6P1 Canada
Phone +1 613 563 4801   Fax +1 613 594 4704
Email: info@interpares.ca   Website: www.interpares.ca

Public Interest Research Centre   PIRC is a research and campaigning group based in Delhi which seeks to serve the information needs of activists and organizations working on macro-economic issues concerning finance, trade and development.

142 Maitri Apartments, Plot No. 28, Patparganj, Delhi 110092, India
Phone: +91 11 2221081/2432054   Fax: +91 11 2224233
Email: kaval@nde.vsnl.net.in

Third World Network TWN is an international network of groups and individuals involved in efforts to bring about a greater articulation of the needs and rights of peoples in the Third World; a fair distribution of the world's resources; and forms of development which are ecologically sustainable and fulfil human needs. Its international secretariat is based in Penang, Malaysia.

121-S Jalan Utama, 10450 Penang, Malaysia
Tel.: +60 4 226 6159   Fax: +60 4 226 4505
Email: twnet@po.jaring.my   Website: www.twnside.org.sg

Third World Network–Africa TWN–Africa is engaged in research and advocacy on economic, environmental and gender issues. In relation to its current particular interest in globalization and Africa, its work focuses on trade and investment, the extractive sectors and gender and economic reform.

2 Ollenu Street, East Legon, PO Box AN19452, Accra-North, Ghana.
Tel.: +233 21 511189/503669/500419   Fax: +233 21 511188
Email: twnafrica@ghana.com

World Development Movement (WDM) The World Development Movement campaigns to tackle the causes of poverty and injustice. It is a democratic membership movement that works with partners in the South to cancel unpayable debt and break the ties of IMF conditionality, for fairer trade and investment rules, and for strong international rules on multinationals.

25 Beehive Place, London SW9 7QR, UK
Tel.: +44 (0)20 7737 6215   Fax: +44 (0)20 7274 8232
Email: wdm@wdm.org.uk   Website: www.wdm.org.uk

This Book is Also Available in the Following Countries

CARIBBEAN

Ian Randle Publishers
11 Cunningham Avenue
Box 686, Kingston 6,
Jamaica, W.I.
Tel: 876 978 0745/0739
Fax: 876 978 1158
email: ianr@colis.com

FIJI

University Book Centre,
University of South
Pacific,
Suva
Tel: 679 313 900
Fax: 679 303 265

GHANA

EPP Book Services,
PO Box TF 490,
Trade Fair,
Accra
Tel: 233 21 778347
Fax: 233 21 779099

MAURITIUS

Editions Le Printemps
4 Club Road
Vacoas

MOZAMBIQUE

Sul Sensações
PO Box 2242,
Maputo
Tel: 258 1 421974
Fax: 258 1 423414

NAMIBIA

Book Den
PO Box 3469
Shop 4
Frans Indongo Gardens
Windhoek
Tel: 264 61 239976
Fax: 264 61 234248

NEPAL

Everest Media Services,
GPO Box 5443
Dillibazar
Putalisadak Chowk
Kathmandu
Tel: 977 1 416026
Fax: 977 1 250176

NIGERIA

Mosuro Publishers
52 Magazine Road
Jericho
Ibadan
Tel: 234 2 241 3375
Fax: 234 2 241 3374

PAKISTAN

Vanguard Books
45 The Mall
Lahore
Tel: 92 42 735 5079
Fax: 92 42 735 5197

PAPUA NEW GUINEA

Unisearch PNG Pty Ltd
Box 320, University
National Capital District
Tel: 675 326 0130
Fax: 675 326 0127

RWANDA

Librairie Ikirezi
PO Box 443
Kigali
Tel/Fax: 250 71314

SUDAN

The Nile Bookshop
New Extension Street 41
PO Box 8036
Khartoum
Tel: 249 11 463 749

TANZANIA

TEMA Publishing Co. Ltd
PO Box 63115
Dar Es Salaam
Tel: 255 22 2113608
Fax: 255 22 2110472

UGANDA

Aristoc Booklex Ltd
PO Box 5130,
Kampala Road
Diamond Trust Building
Kampala
Tel/Fax: 256 41 254867

ZAMBIA

UNZA Press
PO Box 32379
Lusaka
Tel: 260 1 290409
Fax: 260 1 253952

ZIMBABWE

Weaver Press
PO Box A1922
Avondale
Harare
Tel: 263 4 308330
Fax: 263 4 339645